D0482852

ABSOLUTELY EFFORTLESS PROSPERITY

Book II

BY
BIJAN

The Journey Continues
With Another Thirty Simple Yet Profound Lessons
That Will Transform Your Life
In Thirty Days

©1999 by Bijan Anjomi

First Printing 1999
Revised, 2001

All rights reserved. No part of this book may be reproduced or transmitted in any form or by any means, electronic or mechanical, including photocopying, recording, or by any information storage and retrieval system, without permission in writing from the author.

Published by
Effortless Prosperity, Inc.
P.O. Box 370703, Las Vegas NV 89137-0703
Phone (702) 735-6559 Fax (702) 254-0095

ISBN 1-930455-50-X

E-mail Address of Author: bijan@effortlessprosperity.com

This book is available at quantity discounts for bulk purchase.
Study Group discounts also available.

For ordering information:
Call Toll Free: 1-800-437-7750
or visit
www.effortlessprosperity.com/publishing

Cover by Justin Stills and Susan Kallen
Printed in the United States of America

TYDG/SEK

I dedicate this book
to all the wonderful people who have studied
Absolutely Effortless Prosperity Book I
and have seen great miracles and results
in all parts of their lives.

You are now open to receive
Lessons 31 through 60. Shine your light and
be aware of who you really are in every moment.
You are all magnificent extensions of God.

I love you!
My blessing is with you always!

I would like to acknowledge
my guiding angels who have brought this
information through me
for the benefit of all the people on this planet.

I would also like to acknowledge
the wonderful people
who assisted me in bringing forth this book:
Marjorie Lutz, Harriet Tunis, Justin Stills,
Michele Roby and Cory Porter
for their fine-tuning over the years of transition,
Kathy Anjomi for her proofreading,
and Susan Kallen
for final editing , layout and design.

In addition, I would like to acknowledge
Gilda Martin del Campo
for her Spanish translation of
Absolutely Effortless Prosperity, Book I.

My deepest thanks must go to Samia,
who keeps me in joy and light
each moment that I am with her.

And last but not least, I would like to acknowledge
Ted , Dean and Susan
who helped Samia to keep the office operating
effortlessly,
so I could concentrate on writing this book.

Thank You All!

CONTENTS

Always remember Bijan's Law:
Everything that CAN go right
WILL go right.

Expect Miracles!

INTRODUCTION

THE LESSONS

RECOMMENDED READING

xi

INTRODUCTION

*Prosperity
is the ability to be open to receive
all the gifts God has to offer*

*It is the ability to know
that enjoying all the gifts God has to offer
is our natural state of being;
it is our inheritance.*

MESSAGE FROM BIJAN

Most people on this planet think that they are their bodies. Even many very open-minded and spiritual people think that way when they are in fear or pain.

It is not about being wrong or right to think that way, it is about realizing that whenever we think we are the body, then we forget all the powers that we have as a spirit.

As we adopt all the problems of the body, life becomes effortful and full of challenges. The more we adopt this kind of thinking, the more we are convinced that this is who we are. It gets to the point that at the *worst* we argue and complain about our life constantly, and at the *best* we read and learn how to cope with the difficulties that we created out of this kind of thinking. Perhaps we even take a seminar on it from someone who believes in this kind of thinking and is trying to heal himself from that belief system by teaching it.

In truth, we are the creators of our lives, and whatever we believe, we manifest. This life is only a movie: our belief system is the script, we are the producer, we are the director, and we choose our role as the actor or the actors. We have the choice to *change* our role or the script, simply by becoming aware of our thoughts and actions.

My sisters and brothers—when you are in touch with your powers and remember who you are, life is joyous and effortless and magnificent at every moment. You are the highest creation of God, you have all the powers that God has, you are loving and lovable, worthy and deserving, and His wonderful child. Open your eyes, see the truth and act like it.

My deepest wish for each of you is that you remember who you are and start *living* it and *teaching* it—my wish is that you may be a "healed healer".

I love you and I am with you always.
Your loving guide,

Bijan

HOW TO STUDY THIS BOOK

As with *Absolutely Effortless Prosperity Book I*, this book has been designed to be studied one lesson a day. The following are four suggestions that will ensure the best results in thirty days— effortlessly:

- *Remember* that each lesson corresponds to a day of the month, and begin on the first day of any given month with "Day 1, Lesson 31". For the months with more than thirty days, you can simply choose a favorite lesson to read again.

- *Read* the daily lesson and recommended reading immediately upon waking up, and also before going to sleep. Write the lesson on a note card, or even on the palm of your hand, so you will have it available to you all day.

- *Remember* to do the daily assignment.

- *Be open* to receive miracles; share your miracles with others on a daily basis. You may even wish to keep a miracle journal.

Absolutely Effortless Prosperity Book II is a very powerful tool that can take you to a higher level and vibration than ever was available to anyone on this planet. It is important for you to understand that attaining this level will only be achieved when you are complete and comfortable with the lessons from *Book I*. In other words, the time for you to begin studying *Absolutely Effortless Prosperity Book II* is when you know that you are prosperous in every aspect of life, and you enjoy a sense of gratitude in every moment.

As you have learned, prosperity is not measured by the amount of money and power you may have, or even by how good your relationships and health might be. Instead, prosperity is measured by how much joy and peace you feel, in every moment of your life.

If you sometimes find yourself in turmoil instead of in joy and peace, simply be patient with the process; honor it. Take your time with *Absolutely Effortless Prosperity Book I*, and trust that every month you devote to the daily lessons and readings will raise you to a higher level of joy and understanding. And remember: you will know when you are ready for *Book II* by the sense of peace and ease that you feel when you begin it.

These lessons and stories have been written for you, my sisters and brothers, to put you even more in touch with your powers. They will remind you that *you* are in control of everything in your life.

KEEPING YOUR WORD

We are familiar with the black hole in the universe, and we know that whatever passes through it will disappear, or go into a different dimension. What many may not realize is that there is also a black hole within each one of us on this planet.

The black hole within each of us is the place where all God's gifts—the gift of joy, the gift of peace, the gifts of abundance, prosperity, flawless health and loving relationships—get drawn in, before we can embrace them fully. Once these gifts are drawn into our black hole, life for us on this planet becomes struggle, suffering and sacrifice.

Perhaps you are now asking yourself, "What is this black hole?" It is, very simply, *not keeping your word.* Deep inside we know that *God always keeps his word,* and when we do not keep ours, we judge ourselves as not being part of Him—as being *separate.* In believing we are separate from God, we then judge ourselves as being untrustworthy. And in believing we are untrustworthy, we judge ourselves even further as being undeserving of *anything* wonderful that comes from God. So you see, all of our beliefs in suffering, sacrifice, guilt and sin are the result of being drawn into the black hole of *not keeping our word*—of forgetting that we were created by our Creator and are exactly like Him.

It is very important to understand that the degree to which each one of us remembers to keep his or her word, and to cover the black hole, is the degree to which each of us will keep God's gifts that are available for us at every moment. If you have followed the daily lessons of *Absolutely Effortless Prosperity Book I* completely and vigilantly, then you will already have been covering that black hole within you—and your life is now about joy, peace and ecstasy.

Remember to keep your word
at every moment

RECOGNIZING THE TRUTH
IN EVERY EVENT

When incidents bringing joy and happiness come into our lives, we know beyond a shadow of a doubt that they are there to bless us. What we forget is that *every* event only comes into each of our lives to bless us.

Lesson 4 of *Book I* reminds us that we do not know the real meaning of what we see. Any time that we see an event as an attack upon us, and react to it with fear and attack, we create more events that seem to be attacks upon us. This becomes a vicious cycle. Unless we always see the profound truth—that every event is here only to bless us—we are not able to recognize the blessing within every event.

This truth has been manifested and written at the end of each daily lesson in *Book II*, so we may bring light to our minds throughout each day. It is there to help us in remembering that perception is really deception, and things are hardly ever the way they seem. Ego has no creating power, so whatever comes forth, comes from the spirit of God. That is why—at every moment, in every event—we always recognize the profound truth, and say—

this is here only to bless me.

SHARING YOUR MIRACLES
WITH THE WORLD

In *Book I*, you learned that miracles are a natural occurrence—they are expressions of unconditional love. You also learned that when your flow of love has been blocked, and the turmoil of ego has taken its place, miracles do not seem to be happening in your life. Remember that miracles are created by a shift in perception. They occur when you ask Spirit to help you to see through Spirit's eyes, rather than through the eyes of ego.

As you study this book, you will notice that you are opening to receive more and more miracles every day. As you receive them, please remember that it is not only the miracles, but also the *sharing of miracles* that is important. Sharing them on a daily basis will heal any emotions of separation, fear, guilt and anger that you may have. Remember to share your miracles with the world. In sharing them, you empower yourself to be open to receive even more.

THE
LESSONS

God is on the job,
so you don't need to be.
Please relax,
let fear go,
and be happy.

Special Note: Whenever you feel unbalanced, become disturbed, or experience any kind of turmoil, reread the Introduction, to bring you back to peace. And always remember to say, "This is here only to bless me."

11

SPIRIT SPEAKS THROUGH ME

I know the part of me that is real is the child of God, which is unconditional love. Knowing this truth, I am aware that every word I speak is a reflection of Spirit. *Today and every day I choose to speak only words that flow from the unconditional love within me—where peace, light, and truth exist— because this is who I really am.*

RECOMMENDED READING
Limitless Thinking (p. 45)
A Message For Peter (p. 47)

ASSIGNMENT FOR DAY 1
Give a sincere compliment to at least one person.

At every event, just say, "This is here only to bless me."

I LISTEN ONLY TO
WHAT BRINGS ME JOY

I am very aware that what I hear affects my mind, which creates my world around me. I also know that when miracles are shared, I experience joy and peace. Joy and peace are all that I choose to bring into my world at every moment. *Therefore, today and every day I am vigilant in listening for the miracles that others share. I feel the happiness of others, and this brings me joy.*

RECOMMENDED READING
Closing The Door To Darkness (p. 49)

ASSIGNMENT FOR DAY 2
Be vigilant for your laughter today.

At every event, just say, "This is here only to bless me."

I SEE THE LIGHT IN MYSELF AND OTHERS

Just as what I hear affects my mind, what I see affects it, as well. I know that my mind is the source of what happens to me and what I believe about myself. When I see only light and love in others, it mirrors back to me who I am. This is my true self who I have always been and will always be. I know that only light and love are real, and I am devoted to this reality, which I share with my sisters and brothers. *Today and every day I see the light in myself and in others.*

RECOMMENDED READING
Aunt Hoori (p. 51)

ASSIGNMENT FOR DAY 3
Silently admire everyone today.

At every event, just say, "This is here only to bless me."

I AM OPEN TO KNOW THE REAL MEANING OF WHAT I SEE

When I open my mind to the guidance of Spirit, the real meaning of what I see comes to me effortlessly. I need *do* nothing to receive this clarity, as *doing* is in the realm of the body; I only need to be open to receive the guidance of Spirit. Once I know and understand this, a sense of peace comes over me. *Today and every day I am open to know the real meaning of what I see.*

RECOMMENDED READING
In Denial Of Denial (p. 55)

ASSIGNMENT FOR DAY 4
Before you make a decision or react to anything, ask yourself, "What do I really desire from this situation?"

At every event, just say, "This is here only to bless me."

DAY 5 ~ LESSON 35

THE LIGHT IS ALWAYS HERE

When I close my eyes to the light—which is the only reality—what becomes real to me is darkness and illusion. The more I feed into this unreality of darkness and illusion, the more real it becomes to me. The truth is that the light has never left; I have simply chosen not to see it. Light, love, and joy are always here. They are one with me; they are who I am. I can close my eyes and be in darkness or open my eyes to the light. At every moment I have a choice. *Today and every day from this moment on, I will open my eyes and see only the light, which is what I am.*

RECOMMENDED READING
The Light (p. 57)

ASSIGNMENT FOR DAY 5
Acknowledge that you are wonderful.

At every event, just say, "This is here only to bless me."

I AM THE LIGHT

As light cannot know darkness, so it is with me. Everywhere I go and everything I touch are blessed with my light and love. As I shine my light and love on all of my sisters and brothers, I bring forth peace, which is my goal—and healing, which is my function. This is the truth I have acknowledged about myself. *Today and every day I am aware of my real identity as a light of the world.*

RECOMMENDED READING
Living The Dream (p. 58)

ASSIGNMENT FOR DAY 6
Look in the mirror and see the light
in yourself.

At every event, just say, "This is here only to bless me."

DAY 7 ~ LESSON 37

I AM PROSPEROUS IN ALL ASPECTS OF MY LIFE

The "I am prosperous" in this lesson, means more than "I have prosperity"—it means that *I am* prosperity. I give generously, knowing that I have no limitations. The more I give, the more I get in touch with who I am. As the Creator, I am *very* prosperous. Prosperity is within me, and it shows up in my life as I contribute to others outside of me. *Today and every day I am very prosperous in all aspects of my life.*

RECOMMENDED READING
Fear About The Future (p. 61)
Past, Present and Future (p. 62)

ASSIGNMENT FOR DAY 7
Acknowledge all the good things
that you have.

At every event, just say, "This is here only to bless me."

DAY 8 ~ LESSON 38

I AM WHOLE AND COMPLETE

Knowing that I am whole and complete gives me the vision to see that all of my sisters and brothers are here to contribute to me. They provide me with what I need in order to experience life fully. This knowledge—and I assure you that it is *knowledge*—allows me to express my feelings of peace and joy to everyone. *Today and every day I know that I am whole and complete.*

RECOMMENDED READING
A Willingness To Remember Who We Are (p. 64)

ASSIGNMENT FOR DAY 8
Let go of your wants and needs
and concentrate on what you have.

At every event, just say, "This is here only to bless me."

EVERYONE DESERVES EFFORTLESS PROSPERITY

Now that I am aware that we are all children of God, and we all deserve effortless prosperity, I no longer see myself as separate from my sisters and brothers. I know that we are all part of the whole, and the whole is both complete and prosperous. This awareness brings me total peace and joy. *Today and every day I realize that everyone deserves effortless prosperity in all aspects of life. That includes me.*

RECOMMENDED READING
Prosperity Awareness (p. 66)
Effortless Prosperity (p. 70)

ASSIGNMENT FOR DAY 9
Wish effortless prosperity for
everyone you see today.

At every event, just say, "This is here only to bless me."

I AM RECEIVING
ALL OF GOD'S GIFTS

Today I choose to thank God for the abundance I am receiving. I know that God is very happy that I am graciously open to receive all the gifts He is sending to me. The more joy, peace, love and effortless prosperity I receive, the happier God becomes. As I share these gifts with my sisters and brothers, more gifts are sent to me. *Today and every day I am receiving all of God's gifts.*

RECOMMENDED READING
Ego's Maze (p. 74)

ASSIGNMENT FOR DAY 10
Imagine your arms wide open to receive abundance and all great things today.

At every event, just say, "This is here only to bless me."

DAY 11 ~ LESSON 41

I GIVE JUST BECAUSE I HAVE

The truth is that I have everything, and that everything is always available to me. However, if I do not remember this truth, then I live my life in scarcity; I believe that I am not enough and that there is not enough in this world. So to prove that I have, I give, and the more that I give effortlessly, the more I receive. This keeps me in touch with the truth about myself—that I am everything and I have everything. *Today and every day I give just because I know I have.*

RECOMMENDED READING
Give To Yourself Because You Are Worthy (p. 75)

ASSIGNMENT FOR DAY 11
Look around and acknowledge how you
are provided for, and bless everything.

At every event, just say, "This is here only to bless me."

LOVE IS MY REALITY

I know, beyond a shadow of a doubt, that I am blessed and surrounded by the love of God. This is my reality. However, I also know that I am very powerful and can just as easily bring forth fear to dwell upon and to believe in. But why would I be willing to choose fear over joy and turmoil over peace? I am much happier when I am surrounded by the reality of love, joy, peace, and flawless health. *Today and every day I choose the reality of love.*

RECOMMENDED READING
What Is Love? (p. 78)

ASSIGNMENT FOR DAY 12
Think of the one you love most
and bring forth this great love within you.

At every event, just say, "This is here only to bless me."

MY MIND IS IN TOTAL PEACE

Peace is the natural state of my mind. There is not a time, a place, or a circumstance in which peace is unavailable to me. I know this and acknowledge it at every moment of the day. Whenever I am confronted with anything that is not peaceful, I step back from the situation and remember that peace is my natural state and my ultimate goal. I need not accept anything less. *Today and every day my mind is in total peace.*

RECOMMENDED READING
Stepping Away From Turmoil (p. 79)
Total Recall (p. 81)

ASSIGNMENT FOR DAY 13
Step away from the noises of the day; release them.
Find your own quiet space, and acknowledge
the peace within.

At every event, just say, "This is here only to bless me."

ONLY WHAT IS BEST FOR ME SHOWS UP IN MY LIFE

Every day my life becomes more effortless. This is because I have replaced the control of ego with the guidance of Spirit. Now I know that *only* what represents my best interest shows up in my life. This knowledge makes it easy for me to trust my sisters and brothers; this trust is growing by the hour. *Today and every day, I look forward to my life, knowing that only what is best for me will show up.*

RECOMMENDED READING
Anyone Will Do (p. 84)

ASSIGNMENT FOR DAY 14
Ask yourself what you desire and then let it go.
The outcome will be what is best for you.

At every event, just say, "This is here only to bless me."

DAY 15 ~ LESSON 45

I AM ETERNAL

I know that I am an eternal spirit and that I live forever. I also know that being in time provides me the opportunity to heal my mind while I grow in the light of my higher consciousness. I use this time wisely. I have all that I need. *Today and every day I am very patient with myself because I know that I am eternal.*

RECOMMENDED READING
I Am Not My Car (p. 87)
Dreaming (p. 93)

ASSIGNMENT FOR DAY 15
Send love to everyone you see or
think about today.

At every event, just say, "This is here only to bless me."

MY THOUGHTS FLOW
FROM MY LOVING FATHER

I am open to receive only the thoughts that flow from my loving Father. I refuse to allow ego's thought system to enter my mind. Because I am completely vigilant for the light, only thoughts of joy are acceptable to me. It is these thoughts that keep me in the present. *Today and every day I am filled with a sense of peace and tranquility, knowing that all of my thoughts flow from my loving Father.*

RECOMMENDED READING
Manifesting Your Thoughts (p. 95)

ASSIGNMENT FOR DAY 16
Welcome your loving thoughts
and release all your dark thoughts.

At every event, just say, "This is here only to bless me."

MY LIFE IS FULL OF MIRACLES

Every moment that I remember who I am, I become aware of all the wonderful miracles occurring in my magnificent life. As I share the miracles with my sisters and brothers, I extend and release them so that I will be open to receive more. *Today and every day I continually thank God for the many miracles I receive.*

RECOMMENDED READING
Working Out In The Gym (p. 98)

ASSIGNMENT FOR DAY 17
Expect a lot of miracles today.

At every event, just say, "This is here only to bless me."

I AM PEACEFUL

My life is peaceful and joyous when I follow the guidance of Spirit. I am grateful to the whole world—to all my sisters and brothers—for the contributions that are being made to my life. I can see very clearly that all my sisters and brothers are going out of their way to bring peace, love, joy, and happiness to me. *Today and every day I am aware that I am given what I need, so I may be in peace at all times.*

RECOMMENDED READING
Who Is The Real You? (p. 100)

ASSIGNMENT FOR DAY 18
Acknowledge your loving light
at every moment.

At every event, just say, "This is here only to bless me."

I AM A LOVING AND LOVABLE CHILD OF GOD

I know that I am a loving and lovable spirit. It is a quality that I share with all of my sisters and brothers. This truth—that I am loving and lovable— becomes obvious to me as it manifests in all aspects of my life. I see it in my prosperity: everyone wishes to contribute to me. I see it in my relationships: they are all holy. I see it in my health: it is flawless. I even see it in my peace of mind, which is complete. *Today and every day I am happy to know that I am a loving and lovable child of God.*

RECOMMENDED READING
One Child Of God (p. 102)

ASSIGNMENT FOR DAY 19
See yourself as a teddy bear,
lovable and cuddly.

At every event, just say, "This is here only to bless me."

FEAR DOES NOT EXIST

Fear is a lack of love. In order for me to be in fear, love—which is my Source—must be absent. Since there is not a time, a place, a state, or a circumstance in which my Source is ever absent from my life, fear must be an illusion. I can believe in this illusion only when I am not in the present. When I give up my belief in fear, I allow the reality of the present moment, where my Source is, to return to me. *Today and every day I know that fear does not exist.*

RECOMMENDED READING
Childhood Fears (p. 105)
Ego And The Snake (p. 108)

ASSIGNMENT FOR DAY 20
Be vigilant for the light today.

At every event, just say, "This is here only to bless me."

DAY 21 ~ LESSON 51

I AM THE LOVE OF GOD

To God, I am His precious child. His loving gaze upon me is as constant as the gift of peace that He offers me, and I am open to receive it. I know the reality of who I am, and this knowledge puts me in a state of ecstasy. *Today and every day I am the love and the joy of God.*

RECOMMENDED READING
Learning Through Joy And Laughter (p. 109)

ASSIGNMENT FOR DAY 21
Notice how everyone wishes to
contribute love to you today.

At every event, just say, "This is here only to bless me."

DAY 22 ~ LESSON 52

I AM SURROUNDED BY UNCONDITIONAL LOVE

God is unconditional love and He is everywhere. If I am not in touch with His love that is within me, He will communicate what is best for me through my sisters and brothers, in situations that occur around me. As I open my vision, I realize that every experience in my life is an opportunity given to me by my loving Father, to support my growth and happiness. *Today and every day I am surrounded by unconditional love.*

RECOMMENDED READING
Unconditional Love (p. 111)

ASSIGNMENT FOR DAY 22
Look beyond everyone's skin to his or her unconditional love.

At every event, just say, "This is here only to bless me."

DAY 23 ~ LESSON 53

GOD TRUSTS ME COMPLETELY

Because I trust God wholly and without question, I know deep within me that He trusts me completely, as well. I perceive every experience within each present moment as a miracle and an opportunity to be aware of my magnificence and the unconditional trust that God has for me. *Today and every day I know that my Father trusts me completely.*

RECOMMENDED READING
Feelings Versus Emotions (p. 113)

ASSIGNMENT FOR DAY 23
Trust everyone today because
you are trustworthy.

At every event, just say, "This is here only to bless me."

DAY 24 ~ LESSON 54

MY SOURCE AND I ARE ONE

Once I remove the secret illusions of guilt, fear and sin from my mind, I can return to the reality of who I am. My Source and I are one. Life is so joyous, peaceful and effortless, that all I have to do is express gratitude to Spirit and to all of my sisters and brothers. *Today and every day my Source and I are one.*

RECOMMENDED READING
You Are Everything (p. 114)

ASSIGNMENT FOR DAY 24
Feel the oneness with everyone you see today.

At every event, just say, "This is here only to bless me."

I AM GRATEFUL
THAT GOD IS IN CONTROL

The reason my life is working perfectly is that I have moved my small ego-self out of the way, and have allowed my higher self to take over. I can remember the conflicts and turmoil I had struggled with daily when I was giving so much of my power to that little ego-self. However, now that my higher self guides my thinking, my life is peaceful and effortless. *Today and every day I am grateful that my higher self is in control.*

RECOMMENDED READING
Letting Go Of The Past (p. 116)
If Only I Could Have (p. 119)

ASSIGNMENT FOR DAY 25
It is in your best interest to give up control today.

At every event, just say, "This is here only to bless me."

I AM BLESSED AS THE CREATOR OF MY WORLD

I realize that I am a very powerful Creator. I know that everything happening in my life is just a shadow—an effect of my own thinking. My thoughts create my world around me, and as I change my thoughts to reflect the light of my Source, I no longer see myself as a victim. I have become very aware of how fortunate and well rewarded I am. *Today and every day I am blessed as the Creator of my world.*

RECOMMENDED READING
Directions In Life (p. 121)

ASSIGNMENT FOR DAY 26
Acknowledge that whatever is happening
is your desire.

At every event, just say, "This is here only to bless me."

THE WILL OF GOD IS MY WILL

My life is wonderful since my will and the will of God have become one. I no longer have to struggle with judgments and decisions, nor do I have to worry about being right, because God knows what is best for me at every moment. Now my life is filled with peace and joy. Everything I hope for and dream about is showing up effortlessly. *Today and every day I follow the will of God at every instance.*

RECOMMENDED READING
Everyone Is In His Perfect Place (p. 123)

ASSIGNMENT FOR DAY 27
Acceptance is in order today.

At every event, just say, "This is here only to bless me."

I SEE UNCONDITIONAL LOVE EVERYWHERE

As I look around, I see the effect of unconditional love in everyone and everything. I see the kindness and affection of my Source reflected in the eyes of my sisters and brothers, and the peace and joy of my Source in their loving acts. I know that everyone and everything are here to show me that I am appreciated, loved, and taken care of by my all-powerful Source. *Today and every day I see only unconditional love everywhere.*

RECOMMENDED READING
Creating From Conscious Thought (p. 125)

ASSIGNMENT FOR DAY 28
Notice flowers, smiling people, and
all beautiful things today.

At every event, just say, "This is here only to bless me."

I ACKNOWLEDGE MY HIGHER SELF

I acknowledge the self that is within me, and know that the self is one with my Source. My higher self is greater than my body, my thoughts, or even my imagination. It is so incredibly vast that nothing on Earth can hold or contain it. *Today and every day I know and acknowledge my higher self, which is the all-powerful Source of the universe.*

RECOMMENDED READING
The Right Choice (p. 127)
Where Do We Go After The Body (p. 128)

ASSIGNMENT FOR DAY 29
Love yourself today.

At every event, just say, "This is here only to bless me."

DAY 30 ~ LESSON 60

I AM CONSTANTLY COMMUNICATING WITH UNCONDITIONAL LOVE

The communication between unconditional love and myself is so open and clear that I can feel, see, hear and know the truth about everything at every moment. This truth brings such a sense of peace, joy and tranquility to me, that everyone I meet can see it in my eyes. This is the life I have been wishing for; this is the joy I have been praying for. And now that I have unconditional love, I am joyfully looking forward to experiencing every moment of it. *Today and every day I am constantly communicating with unconditional love.*

RECOMMENDED READING
Oneness (p. 130)
Ace In The Hole (p. 132)

ASSIGNMENT FOR DAY 30
Talk and listen to the Spirit within.

At every event, just say, "This is here only to bless me."

RECOMMENDED READING

*A miracle
is always available.*

*When you do not experience it,
you are looking
in the wrong place.*

LIMITLESS THINKING

It is very important for us to be aware of our belief system at every moment, because it manifests whatever is in our lives. The words that we say, and those that we listen to comfortably and effortlessly, are the effects of our belief system.

It is impossible to be prosperous *effortlessly* if we have beliefs of "easy come, easy go—no pain, no gain—you have to struggle to get ahead—you have to pay your dues in life". We have all heard these types of sayings, and many of us have spoken these or similar words without even thinking about where they might have come from.

Originally, these beliefs about acquiring power and money were created by people with strong ego and fear; then as time went by, others *bought into* their belief systems, replacing limitless thinking with self-limiting beliefs. And today, as these false and limiting beliefs continue to be passed on, they are like magnets that pull us away from our natural state of *creating in joy,* and keep us stuck to Earth.

I am always puzzled when I hear a person say that nothing good comes easily, and then I hear that same person complain in the next breath about someone else who has everything coming to him easily and effortlessly. It is puzzling to me, and is *really confusing for the universe.*

First the universe brings forth what the self-limiting person is asking for, which is to have nothing good come easily. Then it hears the person complain about having nothing good come easily, comparing himself to someone with limitless thinking who has everything coming to him effortlessly. In the end, to please the self-limiting person by allowing his conflicting beliefs to be "right", the universe manifests that the person does *not* get what is desired, even after working hard for it.

So, not only do we have to watch what we *say* because we manifest it, but also we also have to be vigilant for what we *listen to and agree with,* for that manifests, too. We must always remember that as long as we have even a single contradictory thought about attaining prosperity effortlessly, we will be unable to attain it.

Truth can still be found in babies and young children who have not yet bought into our limiting belief system; they get whatever they desire, without having to do anything about it. Think of them, and remember that you also came to Earth as a limitless being. Remember this, and be vigilant for undoing—for replacing self-limiting beliefs with the limitless thinking you were born with. There is nothing that you can learn that will bring you closer to the light; only *undoing* will accomplish that.

A MESSAGE FOR PETER

When this book was first published, I facilitated an Effortless Prosperity study group at six o'clock every evening. It was a large group—anywhere from thirty to seventy people—but I was familiar with all of the students.

During my usual meditation one morning, my guide said that he had a message for one of the study group participants. "Tell Peter to use Effortless Prosperity to receive light, not business," he instructed me.

I clearly understood these words, for I had noticed that whenever Peter shared his miracles they always had an underlying message about his business. He often talked about darkness, complaining about his need for more clients. I told my guide that I was aware of what Peter was doing, but was uncomfortable about mentioning it to him. "Just pass on my message—don't judge it," my guide said. Reluctantly, I agreed to do this.

Before class began that evening, I found Peter and gave him the message. His calm response surprised me. He simply said, "Okay," and thanked me. I noticed that when he shared his miracles with the class that evening, he only shared about the light; he never even mentioned his business.

The next evening at class, Peter told the study group about the actual message he had received from my guide the evening before—about sharing only light. Peter continued, saying that when he had been given the message, he had immediately let go of trying to get business from people in the Effortless Prosperity classes—and in letting go, he found that he was overwhelmed with new clients the next day.

For the next two weeks, Peter shared miracles of his tremendous increase in business, of how much money he was receiving, and how his prosperity was pouring in effortlessly. Through his miracles, Peter realized that prosperity came to him easily when he was vigilant for the light—and when he was truly open to receive.

CLOSING THE DOOR TO DARKNESS

While you are following the principles of *Effortless Prosperity*, it is very important that you stay vigilant for the light. By keeping the lessons of the day in your awareness at each moment, you will not only open your mind to receive light, but you will also extend light outward.

Overall, you will be going through stages of healing and growth during the entire thirty-day program, and you will wish to avoid anything that could interrupt the process. In other words, you will wish to close the door to darkness. This could involve changing some things that you normally do.

For example, it would be a good idea to ignore the news, as well as anyone or anything else that is filled with turmoil, violence and other values of the ego. Just as you would wish to stay away from a cold draft when you are getting over the flu, you will wish to stay away from darkness while you are letting go of ego.

At the end of your thirty-day experience, you will be in so much peace—you will be so attuned to Spirit and your guides—that you will immediately know whether something brings you peace or turmoil. At this point, many of the things that you had temporarily avoided will no longer be of interest to you.

But if you do wish to resume watching the news, only do so if you are able to change your perception of it by closing the door to darkness. In other words, watch the news but do not be affected by it. This means you must be strong enough—and open enough—to know that the darkness occurring in this world does not mean anything. In truth, we are all one, and all of us are experiencing the lessons that we have chosen to experience in this lifetime.

AUNT HOORI

Shortly after my mother's death, I began to think a lot about her youngest sister, Aunt Hoori. She was the only aunt who was left. Though we had not stayed in close contact over the years, Aunt Hoori had always been my favorite aunt; now that my mother was gone, I hoped to share with her some of the love and joy that I had shared with my mother. I decided that I would call her at seven o'clock every Sunday morning, on my way to the gym.

I was really excited about the idea of having Aunt Hoori in my life every week, but after talking to her that first Sunday, I was depressed. My energy was depleted. Her whole conversation had been about how miserable her life was and how horrible her health was. She had even complained about the weather! I decided not to call her again for a couple of months.

The second time I called her, our conversation was the same. She complained about everyone and everything. "What has happened to my favorite aunt?" I wondered. I really missed my mother, and had wished to feel some of that closeness with Aunt Hoori, but this was not going to work.

I decided to ask my guide what to do, explaining that I really loved my aunt, and wished to stay in touch with her, but hearing all of that darkness was simply too depressing. My guide laughed and said, "Why are you telling me this? You should be telling her—I can't do anything about it."

"But I don't want her to get upset and stop loving me," I replied. "Besides, I think it would hurt her."

"Your Aunt Hoori is a child of God," he said. "She will never get hurt when you tell her the truth and bring her to the light. Her ego might get hurt, but if you are worried about making her ego unhappy, then you are thinking from *your* ego. Give up wishing to look good and wishing to be loved, and just be vigilant for the light. You will never lose your aunt's love by being vigilant for the light."

I called Aunt Hoori the following Sunday. As soon as she started to complain, I stopped her and said, "Aunt Hoori, you have always been my favorite aunt, and I love you very much, but I don't wish to hear all of this darkness. When all you do is complain, it brings my energy level down."

"I'm simply telling you the truth about what is going on in my life," she said.

I explained that even though her life may be that way, I did not wish to hear about it. She became very quiet. I asked her if there was anything else that she would like to talk about. There was another moment of silence, and then she said no.

Hanging up the phone, I was sad that things had not gone the way I had hoped.

When I called her the following week and asked how she was doing, she said, "Just fine." I asked if there was anything she wanted to talk about, and she said, "Well, you already told me that I shouldn't talk about anything that might upset your day, so I choose to be quiet."

I started to laugh. "Aunt Hoori! Have you been holding that against me all week?" I asked.

"It's not that I'm holding anything against you," she replied, "it's just that I don't want to upset your day."

I thanked her and told her how much I appreciated that. Then I said, "Let me tell you a joke I heard recently." She laughed at the joke I told her, and I thought to myself, "You're making progress, Bijan!" I told her another joke, and then another, and by this time, Aunt Hoori was laughing hard. Before we hung up for the week, I gave her some good news about myself, and shared about how magnificent my life was. As we said goodbye, we both had with smiles in our voices.

I called her every Sunday after that, and as time went by, she opened up to the light more and more. One week my brother even called to tell me he had just talked to Aunt Hoori, and she had told him that she always counted the minutes until I called her on Sunday mornings, because the time she spent on the phone with me was the highlight of her week. "During the call I don't worry about anything! I just laugh and enjoy myself," she had said.

Like so many people, Aunt Hoori had believed that the more miserable her life seemed to others, the more love she would receive from them. She had believed that people would see her as a good person and would extend sympathy to her, because even though her existence was so horrible, she was coping with it so bravely. But slowly, through our weekly phone calls, she had begun to realize that *joy comes from sharing light, not darkness.* And by sharing the light while she was talking to me, she knew that she was taken care of.

Our weekly phone calls have continued for several years, and in all that time she never shared one speck of darkness with me. After we talk every Sunday morning I feel very joyous. I have a wonderful aunt who extends so much love and light that I feel blessed to have her in my life.

IN DENIAL OF DENIAL

Every day I work out at the gym. I know a lot of people there and usually greet them with, "Good morning, how are you doing?" Instead of saying that they are great or not so good or okay, what I usually hear is something like, "Oh, it's Monday," or, "Thank God it's Friday!" The day of the week seems to play a significant role in how they feel. Whenever I am asked how I am doing, I always answer, "Excellent."

One morning I saw a psychiatrist friend of mine at the gym. When she asked me how I was, I told her I was excellent, the way I always do. "Bijan," she said, "I have to give you some advice." Curious about what my friend wished to tell me, I stopped my workout "You are in denial," she announced. Her diagnosis surprised me, and I asked her why she thought that way. "Three reasons," she said. "First, because you *always* say that you are excellent; second, because you are *always* happy, and third, because there is no such thing as *always* being happy."

I thanked her for her advice and continued my workout, but as soon as I returned home, I went right to my meditation table. My guide appeared quickly, asking me what was wrong, and I explained what my friend, the psychiatrist, had told me about being in denial.

"She is right," he said. "From the way she looks at the world, you are absolutely in denial. However, you must realize that she has forgotten who she is, and doesn't know that she is coming from her ego. The truth is that *she* is the one who is in denial. She is denying her oneness with you and with all of her sisters and brothers—and she is denying her own magnificence. Furthermore, she has been in denial for so long that the path she is on looks normal to her. Because this is her reality, it follows that she judges anyone who is not on her path to be in what she considers as denial."

My guide continued. "Bijan, my son, by denying that you are a miserable creature, a victim, or a body filled with fear, you take your place as a guiltless child of God—an extension of your Source. You know who you are, and because of that, you are *in denial of denial*. In time, when your friend has had enough misery and darkness, she will begin to look for the light in herself and others."

Hearing his explanation, I felt much better. And now, whenever I see my friend the psychiatrist, I send her joy and light, and remember only her magnificence.

THE LIGHT

My guide said, "I give you the light and you pass it on in so many ways. Some people are clear and free; the light goes *through* them, and it is passed on to other people. The light will affect those other people too, bringing them into higher vibration, energy, and light."

"Some people have problems with themselves and with you," he continued. "They don't allow the light to go any further than themselves, and the light dies within them. It does not bring them into higher vibration. Those people *stop* the light."

My guide concluded by saying, "It is not my choice or your choice where the light goes, but it is our choice to shine it or not. Whoever is clear, like glass, will let the light pass through them; the light will die in whoever is unclear."

LIVING THE DREAM

While studying the Koran, the Torah, the Bible, and the Baha'i faith, I learned that many prophets of the holy books were more concerned with expressing the truth than with protecting themselves. In fact, they were *so* vigilant for the truth that nothing else —not even their bodies—mattered to them.

I asked my guide about this one morning, during meditation. "I knew that you were going to ask this question," he said. "This was why you had that dream last night. Do you remember it?"

The dream came back to me, vividly. I had been playing, but playing very carefully, so that I would not get hurt. As I was having the dream of playing so carefully, my son had interrupted my sleep by wandered into our kitchen, which was close to my bedroom. This had awakened me slightly, to the point where I was *aware* that I was dreaming. Suddenly my attitude changed; instead of playing carefully and being fearful of my safety, I became very brave. I began to fly around the planet Earth, looking at all the things I had always wanted to see.

I was really enjoying myself, but thought that it would be even nicer if there were others to share this beauty with me. Flying was so much fun that I wished for *everyone* to experience it.

At first I invited only a few people to join me; then a few more came along, and eventually, hundreds of us were flying together, and having a great time. Whenever a new person asked me if he might end up falling out of the sky, I laughed and assured him that everyone was safe; no one should have even a thought about falling. "We are all just dreaming," I kept saying. "We are here to have fun."

And so it continued. We flew all over the planet, enjoying every moment and inviting more people to fly with us, until the group was too large to count. We were all having such a wonderful time! Then I woke up.

"I remember the dream—every detail of it," I said to my guide. "It was very joyous!"

"Bijan," he replied, "now you understand why the prophets and all of the messengers did not care about worldly things—not even about their own bodies. They were aware that this world is only a dream, and there is no need to hold back or play it safe." My guide explained further, "The goal or function of each prophet and messenger has always been to bring all the people to a state of awareness where they, too, can know that this world is *not* reality. This planet is simply a place we have chosen to be upon for a while, where we are meant to live life in joy and gratitude."

I understood what he was telling me. Coming to this planet is not about being safe. We don't have to light matches to see where we have been or where we are going. We are not small, insignificant creatures, but great beings who have come here with the light of the sun in our hands, to light up the world. And we show others—who may not realize it—that they have the light of the sun in their hands, as well. They only have to be willing to see it.

"Beloved brother," my guide said, "you are not here to receive light; you are here to shine the light that you are. When you get in touch with the self that is within you, you will light up the whole world. And the sooner that you and your sisters and brothers do this, the sooner we can all go home to our Source, where we will celebrate our joy together."

I now understood, vividly, the true meaning of my dream and the stories in the holy books.

FEAR ABOUT THE FUTURE

Effortless Prosperity teaches that the future is always about fear. I really desired to understand this concept, so I decided to use one of my real estate deals as an experiment. The deal was in escrow at the time and was supposed to close in thirty days.

I thought about all of the positive aspects of the transaction. First, it had happened very effortlessly; second, I knew that I was going to make a lot of money; and third, it had been a good experience.

But then, suddenly, the thought came to me that perhaps it wouldn't close—that something might go wrong. Immediately, I was filled with fear. "Wow, that was quick!" I thought. It was amazing how quickly my fear had manifested when I had thought about the future.

Now I understood *Effortless Prosperity's* teaching. The past and the future are illusions created by the ego to keep us believing in guilt and fear. As children of God, our only *true* reality is the present. In the present, there is no guilt from the past or fear of the future. So when we live in the present— where our Source is—our lives are filled with joy and peace.

PAST, PRESENT AND FUTURE

It is important for everyone to know that in this lifetime we only have one past and one present, but we have billions of futures. Our future can and will change at every moment, based on the choices, thoughts and actions that we make in the present time.

When we are stuck in a strong belief system that comes from the past, our thought system and choices are very limited. In this case, our past determines our future and we believe we have no choice in the present to change our future. Some people call that karma, which is one hundred percent truth when we do not remember that we always have a choice in the present.

I am *very* aware of this gift from God of having choice in the present, and when thoughts of separation come up—which are always based on fear—I pause and ask myself, "Do I truly desire to create this kind of future, or am I willing to let it go and bring forth love and thoughts of oneness, so my future will be filled with joy and peace?" I grant you that my ego—which is always concerned about the guilt of the past and the fear of the future—will shout and insist for me to pay attention to other people's wrongdoings, and how they treated me badly and I am only a victim here, and so on. But I know better.

I remember that I am a Creator in my own life. If I do not like the path that I am on, I can choose a different path, simply by acknowledging what happened, releasing it, and then choosing a new path for myself.

It is very important for you to become in touch with what I am talking about when I use the words, "acknowledge" and "release". What I mean is that you *let go of* thinking, analyzing, talking about or make a juicy story of whatever has happened. If someone asks you about it, simply answer, "It was an experience which I wished to have at the time; I am complete with it now, so there is nothing to talk about anymore."

Now be in the present and know that you have the choice to have any kind of future that you desire. The question is always, "Where are you going, and what do you desire? Peace or turmoil. Love or fear." You choose.

A WILLINGNESS TO REMEMBER
WHO WE ARE

While here on Earth, our goal is to become aware of our oneness with everyone and everything. Before there was the thought of separation, our only thought was the oneness that we shared with God and with everyone else. We knew that we were a part of the whole, and that the whole was all of us. With this knowledge, we supported and contributed to each other, sharing our love and joy in a state of peace and ecstasy.

After ego was formed, however, all of this changed. With ego came thought of separation. We began to think individually. Our thoughts became private and secretive; we formed our own viewpoints. And, since ego thrives upon comparison, we began to judge and evaluate, which produced thoughts of jealously, anger, and resentment.

Each mind believed that it was self-sufficient and separate from every other mind. Dark thoughts began to enter in, and the stronger ego became, the more darkness there was. This false sense of separation from one another, and from God, gave rise to the belief in guilt. And the guiltier we believed we were, the greater our fear became. So, where we once had known ourselves to be mighty beings who were joined with others as part of the whole, ego now had us believing we were small, scared, and cut off from everyone and everything.

Unfortunately, we cannot kill the ego. But we can integrate it, breaking down the wall of guilt and fear that we have built. One way we can integrate the ego and break down the wall is by joining our minds with other minds. When we share our individual and secret thoughts, they lose their reality and their effect. Another way we can break down this wall is by bringing our dark thoughts to the light. Whenever we shine light on darkness, fear simply disappears. Each of these ways helps us to heal our false sense of separation from one another and from God; the more healing that occurs, the more we become aware of our *oneness* with everyone and with God.

Some people actually think that *they like their wall and separation,* not realizing this is only their ego's belief system put into action. In truth, real freedom, power, peace, and joy come from *knowing our oneness* with everyone and everything. It is from this oneness that we can each create and manifest a magnificent life. All that is needed is a little willingness—a willingness to remember who we really are.

PROSPERITY AWARENESS

When I first met Dr. James, we instantly became close friends, and talked for several hours. During this conversation he told me he was going to die soon. "I can only survive for another six months," he said.

I was very disturbed by his statement, and asked him what incurable disease he had. He explained that it was not a disease that would kill him; he was going to die of hunger because of his financial situation. When I asked Dr. James if I could help out with some money or food, he laughed and said, "No, I'm okay for now—it's the future that I'm so worried about."

A couple of days later, as we were driving down the Pacific Coast Highway, Dr. James pointed out a beautiful cliff overlooking the beach in Laguna, California. "I own that piece of land," he told me in a matter-of-fact voice.

I was a bit puzzled. "You mean the bank owns the land and you have to pay a huge loan payment on it every month," I said.

"No," he replied. "I paid for it with cash. But what really bothers me is that I have to pay property taxes of $120 on it every month."

Hearing him say that left me even more puzzled. I offered to do a financial statement on his holdings, certain this would help him feel secure enough that he wouldn't believe he was going to die of hunger in six months. He accepted my offer. Immediately we returned to his office, where he supplied me with all of the information that I would need.

Later that day, I researched his records from the title companies to see what he owned and what he owed. Surprisingly, I learned that he was quite well off.

The next day I told him that if he signed a power-of-attorney form over to me on the properties that he owned, I would sell them all within six months. He would earn $600,000—and that was *after* my ten-percent commission. I explained to him that I would be "force selling" the properties, for much less than they were worth. This way, they would sell much faster and he would be at peace.

Dr. James was very surprised and didn't believe me at first. I went over all the numbers with him and explained them in detail. Finally, he accepted that what I had told him was the truth, and seemed to be quite happy. "So maybe I won't die from hunger after all," he said. "Perhaps I have underestimated my financial position." He told me that he felt comfortable with things as they were, and decided not to sell.

But within a few weeks he had forgotten everything I had explained to him, and was again insisting that he was going to die of hunger. Patiently I reminded him of his holdings, going over the numbers once again. As before, he accepted what I told him and felt comfortable.

After that, I saw him about every three months over a period of several years. The story was always the same: he was going to die of hunger within six months. Each time he said that, I would remind him of how well off he was. We would talk for an hour or two, and by the end of the conversation he would be happy again. But his happiness was always short-lived, and he would return to his old thoughts of scarcity.

The last time I saw Dr. James, and listened to him replay his sad story, I couldn't help myself. I just started to laugh. He was very upset about my reaction, and became even more vigilant about his belief of dying from hunger.

He was so upset when we parted that I decided to check on the current status of his financial situation. What I discovered was that over the past several years he had lost *everything* he owned. He had literally manifested his greatest fear—which he had unconsciously wished upon himself—and was living from paycheck to paycheck.

I was still disturbed by the whole thing the next morning, so I asked my guide how this could have happened to my friend Dr. James. My guide said, "If you have a million dollars in a savings account and you forget that it is there, in your mind you don't have it. It's not that you have lost it, but that you have just forgotten about it. See, if you do not know what you have, then you do not believe that you have it."

"And so it is with the gifts from God," he continued. "You will never lose them, but you have forgotten that you have them. God has given you everything. All that you have to do is be open to receive. People like Dr. James are so filled with the belief in scarcity that they never think they have enough. And since they are very powerful and are the creators of their own world, it is only a matter of time before they manifest their fears."

EFFORTLESS PROSPERITY

One day as I was warming up in the gym while waiting for my workout partner Danny, I noticed a tall macho-looking guy with a thick mustache, a ponytail and tattoos covering most of his body. He was wearing baggy black leather pants and a tank top, and did not look very happy. I thought to myself, "Where this guy comes from, he must be a gang leader or something."

Then I remembered my agreement with myself. "Oh no," I thought. "I am judging this man and now I have to go and talk to him to clear my judgment."

I was not very happy about this, but I knew I had to keep my agreement. Ego came up several times with excuses for me not to do any thing about it, but each time I heard my guides quietly saying, "Just keep your agreement."

Finally I walked to the mustached man with the tattoos, put out my hand and said, "Good morning, my name is Bijan."

He showed his white teeth with a big smile and said, "Good morning to you! My name is Jeff. It's nice to meet you!" After some small talk, he asked me what I did for a living. When I told him I was in real estate and worked mostly in land, he raised his eyebrows and said, "That's amazing! I work with

70

the president of Del Webb in Las Vegas. We ride Harley Davidsons together, too," he added. "If you like, I'll connect you with him, and maybe you can do business." I was delighted by this opportunity, because Del Webb was one of the biggest and finest developers in the country. We exchanged phone numbers and I went back to my workout.

It was not long before my partner showed up. We got right into our workout, and somewhere in the middle of it, I said, "Danny, you are so friendly—it seems that you know everyone in town. Is there anyone you *don't* know?"

"Not really," he said with a laugh. Then he thought for a while and said, "Well, there is *someone* in this town I have been trying to connect with for a couple of years, but somehow *nobody* can get to him."

"Well if you can't get to him, no one can!" I said with a laugh. Then I asked, "Who is this guy?"

"The president of Del Webb," he answered.

It took a few minutes for me to connect this to my earlier talk with Jeff, but finally I said, "I think I can get you in." Danny gave me a disbelieving look and we dropped the subject.

The next day I called the number for the president of Del Webb. His secretary said he was expecting my call, and put me through to him right away. He was very pleasant with me, and told me to call a man named Mr. Johnson, who was their head of all Las Vegas real estate. He said that he had just hired Mr. Johnson and had already told him about me. I thanked him and called Mr. Johnson, making an appointment to have lunch with him the next day.

I took Danny to the restaurant with me the next day. Mr. Johnson showed up on time, and the two made a great connection. On the way out I told Mr. Johnson that he would be working directly with Danny from then on; he agreed and we left.

At that moment I had no idea if any thing was going to come out of the lunch meeting, and even if it did, Danny and I had no written agreement that he should give me a percentage of anything. A few of my friends in real estate told me, "You had better get all agreements in writing or you will not get anything from him." But I trust God completely, and I know that God is everywhere, so that means I also trusted Danny completely. I knew that everything always works out the way that is best for me.

The most important thing for me was that every time I thought about this deal, I felt very much in peace about the whole thing. That is why I knew it was going to be okay. I blessed it, and I simply let go of the outcome.

Several months later, Danny handed me a large check. He explained that he had put together a large land deal between one of his clients and Del Webb, and chose to give me half of all the commissions coming to him from this deal. "This check is only half of what you will receive," he said. "The rest will be paid over the next three years."

I was very happy and thankful, and knew that whenever I let go of control, trusting God and my sisters and brothers, everything becomes totally effortless.

EGO'S MAZE

Ego's way out is like going deep into a maze. Whenever we have problems and ask ego to help us, ego's solution is to go deeper into the maze. If we continue listening to ego, we go so deep that it feels as though there is no way *out* of the maze—there is no light at the end of the tunnel.

When we are this deep into the maze, listening to God's voice is a struggle. We are confused, and again we listen to ego instead of to God's voice. And so, ego leads us even *deeper* into the maze. Finally, we are so deep that the only way out is just to stop listening to ego—and to trust God totally. If we ask God, He will show us the way out.

But sometimes when we are so deep in the maze, God's way appears to be leading us *away* from the exit of the maze—*away* from freedom—rather than *toward* it. At times like those, we trust God to know that His way is the only way to get out of the maze. Letting go of ego and trusting God totally is the only way out. As long as we follow the voice within us that comes from our heart, our peace, and our love, we are following God's voice.

GIVE TO YOURSELF BECAUSE
YOU ARE WORTHY

It is very important that we freely give to others. Any time that we spontaneously give gifts to others or spend money on them without any judgment, we support within ourselves the fact that we are prosperous. The more that we give and spend, the more that our prosperity manifests.

It is also very important that we freely give to ourselves. In doing this, we are saying, "I am *worthy*; I *deserve* prosperity." When we do not give to ourselves, we are into self-sacrifice; in essence, we are telling ourselves and the universe, "I am *unworthy*; I do *not deserve* prosperity."

Before I became aware of my own prosperity and abundance, I was very much into self-sacrifice. I had come from Persia—which is now known as Iran—and self-sacrifice was all I knew. Though I had become a millionaire and was very generous to my family, I was still uncomfortable about spending money on myself. But finally, after an experience I had with my brother-in-law, the door to prosperity consciousness began to open for me.

For some time, my brother-in-law and I had been talking about buying fishing boats for ourselves. Although he did not have much money in the bank, he still decided to buy himself a beautiful new $17,500 boat, and immediately began to enjoy it on the lake.

I eventually bought a fishing boat, too, but I only allowed myself to spend $450 for mine. The boat I chose was very run-down, and it seemed to be breaking down constantly. Even after spending another several thousand dollars for repairs on it, I often found myself sitting helplessly in the middle of the lake, stranded.

This experience taught me the lesson that I needed. Prosperity doesn't have anything to do with how much money you have; prosperity has to do with how you *feel* about yourself. If you know that you are worthy, and you are willing to spend money on yourself, then prosperity and abundance will *always* be available to you. I knew that my brother-in-law did not have very much money in the bank, yet I now realized that he was very prosperous.

It is important to remember that there is a lesson in every experience and in every situation. If we go within and ask, "What is the lesson for me?" we will be told—and we can walk away from the experience richer *and wiser*. However, if we are coming from our egos, we will see ourselves as victims. The emotions of jealousy, anger, and fear will rob us of the perfect lesson that we might have had the opportunity to learn.

I am so happy that I was able to go inside and ask what the lesson in this boat experience was for me. In doing so, I saved myself from all of those negative emotions I might have felt toward my brother-in-law.

And now, whenever I think of him and his boat, I bless him. Through him, the magnificent door to prosperity consciousness began to open for me.

WHAT IS LOVE?

Love is a state of being that we become aware of when we are in total acceptance. It is *who we really are*. When we release all emotions and darkness and illusions, *who we really are* is revealed to us—as unconditional love.

Ego does not understand unconditional love. Ego puts conditions on everything, because everything that ego understands is based upon comparison and judgment. Ego is unable to feel or acknowledge anything; love is totally out of ego's reach. But whenever we let go of the ego's comparison and judgment, we achieve a state of total acceptance and forgiveness. Then the feeling of love comes forth, ego disappears, and we notice that we are again dwelling in love, as love is dwelling in us.

The truth is that only love exists, and ego is an illusion. Ego will disappear in the presence of love, as darkness disappears in the presence of light. What is love? Love is you, when you remember who you really are.

STEPPING AWAY FROM TURMOIL

In one of my meditations, I asked my guide, "Why can't I feel—or even hear—your presence whenever I am experiencing turmoil deep inside of me? Do you dislike turmoil so much that you are unavailable to me when I am in it?"

Before I could say another word, he stopped me. "I must always respect and honor your choices," he said. "When you are in turmoil, you have already chosen not to be in peace. I cannot overpower the decision that you have made for yourself. Turmoil is a heavy blanket that you cover yourself with, so that you cannot hear me or any other guides. We cannot force anything upon you that is against your will or wishes."

"How, then, can I get out of turmoil, so that I can hear your voice and receive your guidance?" I asked my guide.

"Simply step away from the turmoil," he replied. "Mentally and physically, simply step back."

"For example," he said, "if you are sitting on a chair while in turmoil, get up and take one or two steps backward. Imagine and see your turmoil still sitting on the chair. If you are lying down, get up and stand back; imagine and see your turmoil still lying there, where you had been. And if you are standing up, talking to someone or doing something, just step backwards; move away from where you were standing. Imagine and see the turmoil still standing where you were, and realize that you are not in the turmoil anymore."

My guide concluded by saying, "Once you remove yourself from the turmoil, you will feel the peace that surrounds you. Choose *not* to be in turmoil, and then I can come into your mind and give you the answers you are seeking and the light that you are searching for."

I have used this exercise ever since it was given to me by my guide, and it always works. I know that I have the choice to be in turmoil or in peace—to be in ego or in unconditional love.

Like me, you can also use this magnificent exercise to stop ego from playing its game. As long as you are vigilant for the light and step away from turmoil, you will *always* be surrounded by peace.

TOTAL RECALL

I was in an overwhelmingly deep and peaceful meditation one morning when my angel asked, "What do you desire above all?"

I answered without hesitation. "My highest desire is to remember everything, especially starting from when I was with God."

"Before you can do that," my angel said, "you must forget and let go of everything here on this planet."

I understood the task. Blanking out the past and the future, I saw myself standing in the present moment with nothing attached to it. Suddenly I found myself in a deeply calm and quiet place that was extremely peaceful and joyous. In this place I did not know anything, but at the same time I was aware of everything! I was nowhere special, yet I was everywhere! It was a feeling and a sense of *knowing* that I had never felt before.

My angel pointed in a direction for me to look. When I did, I noticed something moving. At first glance it seemed like a ball of light, but as I looked deeper into the ball of light, I recognized myself! I did not appear the way I do now, but I knew it was Bijan. Even though I was here, I was also there!

I loved the feelings of movement and action in this ball of light, and decided to experience them even more—so I divided myself into pieces. I *really* loved that, because I was experiencing movement and action in so many ways, on so many levels—so I continued to divide and subdivide until I was all over! Suddenly I heard my angel say, "Time to come back home, Bijan."

I didn't understand. "Where is home?" I asked.

"Home is the peace that you call oneness," my angel replied. I was not sure about what he meant. Seeing this, my angel said, "It was hard for you to know yourself as everything, so you had to become something separate from everything, in order to have experiences that you desired." I was beginning to understand what my angel was telling me, but asked for more clarity.

"Let me make it very simple for you," he continued. "It is like an African cichlid fish that keeps its newborn babies in its mouth most of the time, for safety. Whenever the babies are outside and feel the fear, they rush back to their parent's mouth right away, for protection."

"Bijan," he said, "you are like the cichlid babies. You have been playing far too long and are tired and worn out. You wish to go back to your Source, but you are so confused that you don't know which way to go. Luckily, though, your deep desire is the same as your Source—it is *the joy of oneness,* whether you are aware that you desire to be in it, or not. However, if you are not aware of it, you will struggle and resist the love of going back to the peace."

As I came out of my meditation, I realized how everything in the universe is only here to contribute to my remembrance of who I am, and of how much I desire to go back to my Source.

ANYONE WILL DO

I was working out at the gym every day with a workout partner. One morning when he did not show up, I started to do the usual workout by myself. After awhile, though, I really began to miss having someone to talk to. Just as I had that thought, I heard my guide's voice say to me, "Anyone will do."

"No, not just anyone," I replied. "It has to be someone I can feel comfortable with—someone who doesn't have judgment toward me."

"Anyone will do," my guide said. "Why don't you talk to the person who is closest to you?"

I looked around, but the only person close to me was an older gentleman with receding hair. I did not have a good feeling about him, so I looked a little further away. There still wasn't anyone to talk to. "Perhaps I should look even further away for someone," I thought.

My guide repeated, "The person who is closest to you will do."

By this time, I was thinking I would rather move to another section of the gym than talk to the gentleman with receding hair. My guide heard my thoughts and said, "Don't move. Just talk to the person closest to you. He will do."

I did not know why I was being so stubborn—my guide had never been wrong in the past. Once again I looked at the gentleman, and though he did not seem happy or friendly, I smiled at him anyway. "Good morning," I said.

He looked up from his workout, smiled back and answered, "Good morning." Then he stopped his workout and just stood there.

For a moment I thought I must have frightened him. I was sure he was going to leave. Instead, he walked over and began to tell me how much he liked this gym, and that he really loved working out here. The gentleman was very enthusiastic and had a great attitude.

Before long, we were working out together and carrying on a warm, friendly conversation. I noticed that he had an accent, and asked him where he was from. When he said he was from Persia, I realized that we had even *more* in common. I felt very comfortable with him, and thoroughly enjoyed our conversation.

From that experience in the gym I received three miracles, which increased my level of awareness.

First, I was shown how wrong my judgments are. If I had listened to my ego, I would have missed meeting this wonderful man who has become a dear friend since that first conversation.

Second, I came to know, on an even deeper level, that we are all spiritual beings. When we are given the opportunity, we truly wish to share our love.

And *third but not least*, I was reminded of how the universe works through my guides. I can always trust them because they have only my best interest in mind.

I AM NOT MY CAR

A few years ago, I went to a party at a friend's house. As I stood talking to some people I knew, I noticed a woman on the dance floor that I had met at the gym. When she saw me, she stopped dancing, waved, and walked over to where I stood.

We talked, laughed and danced together for a while, and then she asked if I would like to go with her to another party across town.   I agreed. As we said our good-byes and left the house, she insisted that we take her car because she did not trust leaving it anywhere. This was not a problem for me; I would simply return for my own car later.

While walking to her car, I noticed an old classic Corvette on the street ahead of us; it looked clean but very run-down. We approached the Corvette and the woman took a handkerchief out of her purse, to wipe the taillight. "Oh no, it looks like this part didn't get washed," she said.

"This woman obviously likes to keep her car clean," I thought to myself. As I moved closer to the car, she moved closer to me.

"Bijan," she said, "I would like you to meet Jodie." Then, she turned slightly toward the Corvette and said, "Jodie, this is Bijan."

I looked at her with surprise and asked, "Jodie? Who is Jodie?"

"Jodie is my car, and she is very precious to me," the woman replied. "I've had her for a long time. We are very close."

I started to feel just a little bit uncomfortable. The woman unlocked the passenger door and said, "Please be gentle with me."

"Wow," I thought to myself as I got into the car, "this relationship is moving a little too *fast*!"

Once seated, I opened her door from the inside and closed mine. "Ouch!" she said.

I thought that the door had accidentally hit her as it was pushed open. "Sorry," I said. "Did I hurt you?"

"No, not me," she replied. "My door. You closed it really hard, and that hurts."

I looked at her and then looked at the door, thinking to myself, "This is getting strange."

We sat in the Corvette for several minutes after the woman started it. "My engine always needs to warm up before I move," she told me. So we waited. It happened to be a very warm evening and I was beginning to perspire.

Once we began to move, I asked her if she had air conditioning. "Yes," she said, "but I don't know if I can take a lot of heat."

"I wasn't talking about you; I was talking about the air conditioner," I said.

"Yes, yes—that's what I mean," she said. "I don't know if my engine can take the heat from the air conditioner being on."

I told her that perhaps it would be better if we took my car. "No, no—it's okay—we can turn the air on," she said. But as soon as the air inside the car cooled down, she turned the air conditioner off again, and said, "It's very hard on me and my engine. I don't know if I can take it any longer."

By now, I was totally bewildered. "What's going on?" I asked her. I didn't know if she was talking about herself or the car.

"I don't know why it's so hard for people to understand how fond I am of my car," the woman complained. "If the engine can't take the heat caused by running the air conditioner, I feel very, very uncomfortable."

The air inside the car was getting hot again, and I asked if we just could go back and get my car.

She agreed to take me to my car, but added that she would still have to drive her Corvette to the party, because she didn't trust leaving it alone.

The woman turned her car around and drove very slowly as she took me back to mine. When I asked her why she was just creeping along, she replied, "I noticed that my engine was getting a little hot, so I have to drive slower, to cool it down."

I understood her concern, but by that time I just wanted to get away from her, so when we got back to the original party, I mentioned that I thought I would like to stay there for a while. She had no problem with my decision, and drove off. Watching her leave, I realized that what I really wanted to do at this point was to go home and meditate on the unusual experience I had just been through.

As soon as I walked into the house, I went to my meditation table. My guide showed up right away—he was laughing, but I was not amused. "Why did that woman see herself as her car?" I asked. My guide explained that this had been a lesson in extremes, to show me how all of us see ourselves as our vehicles. "But I don't see myself as my car," I insisted. "I'm not even interested in my car."

"Not your car," he said. "Your body. Your body is your vehicle, but you forget that it is *just a vehicle*."

"My body is just a vehicle," I said in my mind.

"Yes, Bijan, your body is just a vehicle," he repeated. "It exists simply as a means for you to communicate with other spirits that are also using bodies. You often forget this, and believe that *you* are your *body*. You spend much of your waking time feeding it, pampering it, worrying about it, and doing everything in your power to make it look good—so the experience I gave you tonight was to remind you that *you are not your body*. Your mind can *never* be physical, but it can reach out through your body to extend itself. If your mind is blocked by your body and you believe that you *are* your body, then your mind can become sick."

" The problem with this woman believing that she *is* her car is that she also has all of her car's problems, as you do with your body. These problems are all created by a split mind. But when you realize the wholeness, the oneness, and the magnificence of who you are—and that your body is just a way to communicate this oneness— then your body will have flawless health."

My guide concluded, "You do not need to see your body as any more than what it was created to be: a means to join your mind with the minds of your sisters and brothers in your function of healing and forgiving. When you see this, your body can do its function of serving you in total health, high energy and joy."

Looking back on the experience now, it seems very funny to me. But at the time it happened, it felt strange; I was very puzzled by the woman's behavior. Whenever I think of her, I bless her and pray that she will see herself as separate from her car and one with God.

DREAMING

The dreams that we have, and the games that we choose to play, offer us all kinds of things—up and down, good and bad—but it is all a dream.

Even the parts of the dreams that save us from suffering are still a part of the dream.

We think that dreams are made of good and bad, and we must suffer in order to be saved. We create misery and struggle for ourselves in our lives, so that we can be saved by something like money, power, different relationships, or even health.

When I asked my guide to explain this, he said, "Beloved child, I wish you would remember how excited you were before you came to this world—to this dream—where you would have the opportunity to play this game. Look at you now. You take the game so seriously, thinking you are really *there* and that all these things are *happening* to you."

He continued. "You think all these exciting things that you choose to dream are horrible nightmares, meant to hurt you. But they can be gone with a flick of your finger. They can be gone with the smallest knowledge of who you are. When you know who you are, you know this is nothing but a game for you—a game to play so that you will not get bored."

"You have a choice to be happy *without* a reason," my guide said. "Any *reason* that makes you happy can also make you *unhappy* if you lose it—if you lose the reason. Choose to be happy because you are the beloved child of God—because you are the Creator. You have everything because you *are* everything. Your total happiness must always come from the knowledge of who you really are—not from what you have or do, and not from what you dream about."

MANIFESTING YOUR THOUGHTS

As we follow the lessons of *Effortless Prosperity* every thirty days, we go through several stages.

During the first few months, we get in touch with everything that we have thought of at one time or another in the past, thus manifesting those thoughts.

As we progress through several more months of studying *Effortless Prosperity*, we realize that our present thoughts and wishes can also be manifested very quickly.

Finally, we get to the point where our thoughts manifest immediately. We are now faced with a question: do we really wish to manifest our thoughts immediately, or do we prefer to have a delay in the manifestation so we can think about the thoughts and perhaps cancel them?

I remember the first experience where my thoughts began manifesting very fast—almost instantly. I was driving to Mt. Charleston with my twelve year-old son, Michael; on the way there, I noticed several sparrows flying close to my car, but not touching it. Watching the sparrows, I thought to myself, "I could accept seeing one of those sparrows hit the car." Immediately, a sparrow flew right into the windshield!

Seeing the bird hit the glass, I was suddenly very uncomfortable and confused; I had not realized how quickly my thoughts were manifesting

We finally got to Mt. Charleston, spread a blanket on the grass, and set out a cooler filled with some of Michael's favorite drinks and some of mine. While relaxing on the blanket, I asked Michael to bring me one of my favorite drinks. He reached into the cooler, grabbed one of my bottles, and opened it. But then, instead of giving it to me, he began to drink from it. I was unhappy with this, even though I knew I had more bottles in the cooler.

Again, I asked Michael to get me one of my bottles, specifically asking him not to drink this one. As before, Michael reached into the cooler, grabbed one, opened it, and drank it.

At this moment a strong, dark and angry thought came into my mind. This thought was so strong that I verbalized it—but quietly, so Michael could not hear me.

The moment the words were spoken, my son began choking. He could not breathe, and was beginning to turn blue. I was in a panic, and quickly said, "Cancel that thought!"

Immediately, Michael began breathing again.

Once I knew that my son was okay, I left the blanket and walked into the forest, to meditate. When my guide came to me, I told him that I didn't wish to have my thoughts manifesting that quickly anymore. I explained that I wished to have time to digest my thoughts first, and have the opportunity either to continue thinking them or to cancel them.

I realized that I did not yet have enough mastery to control my thoughts in such a way that they would all be wonderful and positive. Somehow, when I found myself in a moment of anger or fear, ego still seemed to be coming in, bringing dark wishes.

Since that day at Mt. Charleston, my thoughts still manifest, but they do not manifest instantly. Instead I am able to look at them, first—to ensure that they are light, and that they are good for me and for everyone else.

WORKING OUT IN THE GYM

I work out in the gym every day with one or two workout partners. One of them—David—is quite a strong and masculine person. He is very much into his body and looks like an extremely macho guy.

One morning when we were working out together, David took a break to get a drink of water. While waiting for him to return, I looked around the gym and noticed a very spiritual gentleman who had attended my *Effortless Prosperity* seminars in the past. He noticed me, too, and walked toward me with his arms opened wide in joyful recognition. I walked up to him and gave him a strong hug. I felt the oneness with this gentleman.

As we finished hugging, I noticed David returning from his break. Spontaneously, I turned toward him with a wide smile and opened my arms. He gave me a strong hug, but seemed to be looking around the gym in embarrassment. It was extremely crowded that day, not to mention the fact that we were working out on a machine that was facing all the stair-masters.

As I pulled away from David, he turned to the people watching us. "...a spiritual man...a very spiritual man," he said loudly as he patted me on the back.

Then he raised his right hand and asked me to give him a high five. To make him feel more at ease, I grinned and gave him a very *macho* one.

I realized that this must have been an uncomfortable situation for David, as he is not used to hugging anyone—male or female—especially in public. It is very normal for me to hug another person at any time.

WHO IS THE REAL YOU?

You are the Self and the Ever-Present in your life. You were present at your birth, throughout your childhood and your teen years, and you are still patiently waiting to be recognized.

You will never force your way to the front, ever content to let the ego fulfill its desire, running rampant with your experiences. You, the Spirit within—the soul that is connected with the creative power of God—you remain peaceful and content through all of your experiences. You see life as a journey that you have chosen to embark upon.

Your ego was born at your physical birth. Who you are, the being, gives the power to allow the ego to exist. You even allow the ego to judge and evaluate everything. Your ego tells you that you are one with it, and sets its resentment, grievances, anger and fear upon you.

Think: when was the last time that you listened to your ego, bought into its fantasy and wishes, and found that it brought you total peace and joy? Look at your ego with wide-open eyes and notice that its words and advice bring only misery and pain. Ego's talk is always about lacking—always about our relationships being a bit off. It's always about not deserving success, and not being good enough.

You do not have to listen to ego anymore. "Who you are" is the Spirit—the cause—the love within. It is *you* who is the power and the Source, not the ego. Ego is the last choice in this world for anyone to have as a guide.

Someone might hear these words and say, "I already *know* all this, but how do I quiet down the voice of my ego in my mind? How do I *not* listen to it and *not* act on ego's direction?"

The answer is simple. The principles of *Effortless Prosperity* give us direction. The teachings give us a new way of listening to the other voice—the voice that brings us total peace and joy—the voice that comes straight from our Father, from our Source, from our Creator.

All it takes is to be vigilant to the daily lessons all day, every day, for thirty days. Live them.

The result will be evident. You will joyously and gladly begin to hear what you had closed off from the moment you were born, when ego came into your life.

ONE CHILD OF GOD

In conversations with my guides, I have often heard them say, "There is only one child of God, and you are it." I never really understood this concept. So one morning, during a deep meditation, I asked, "How can there be only one child of God when there are *billions* of us on this planet?"

The explanation that one of my guides gave me was remarkable. He brought forth a snowflake-filled glass globe and said, "Outside this dome there is no time and no limit. Everything is known, yet nothing is experienced. But inside, there is a planet called Earth. On Earth, time exists, and everything is bound by it."

He continued, "God had only one child. This child manifested itself on the planet inside the dome, where it lived a long life in time. Let's say this child was called Adam. When there was nothing else the child wished to experience as Adam, he shed his physical body, left the planet and went outside the dome."

"After some time, Adam decided to go back to the planet to play himself as a woman, so that he could have that experience and also have someone to keep him company. So he re-entered the dome and lived a lengthy life as Eve, as well as living as Adam."

"Eventually, however, he left the planet in the dome and returned to God again. But after a while, he thought that he would like to have the experience of being a child in physical form. He re-entered the dome as a child born to Adam and Eve, and experienced life from childhood on."

"Each time he left the planet in the dome and went back to God, he would make the decision to return and take on a new role. And each time that he re-entered the dome to be on the planet, he forgot all of his other roles, so that he might freely experience the new one. And so this went—on and on, experience after experience. And the one child remained the only child, but he manifested himself as many others. When he was out there with God, he knew everything—he was everything—but he couldn't *experience* anything until he manifested on the planet and came into action. And because he desired to have every experience that he could, he continued to be reborn. Now he not only had knowledge, but he also had experience."

"Ultimately," my guide said, "you will know that everyone here is you, and that each person is simply playing a role that you wished to experience. As you look around, you will see yourself everywhere. Accept all of us without judgment. Know that we are all where we are supposed to be, in order for you to have the experience that you wish to acquire."

"As you, we have brought light and we have also brought darkness, but we are neither good nor bad, right nor wrong. We are simply you, experiencing different things as different people at different times."

"When you know this," my guide concluded, "you will stand back and you will simply allow yourself to *be*, so that you can experience all that you desire to experience."

CHILDHOOD FEARS

After moving to the United States at age nineteen, I noticed several changes in my lifestyle. Among them was the fact that I was now showering three or four times a day. It never occurred to me that there might be something wrong with this; I just thought that I wished to be clean.

When I went home to Persia for a visit several years later, my mother and some others in the family found it odd that I showered so many times in one day. Each time someone asked why I was taking so many showers, I simply replied that I liked to be "squeaky clean". Actually, my ego was very proud that I was cleaner than everyone else.

After returning to my home in the United States, I noticed that some of my friends were also beginning to make remarks about my cleanliness—and I wondered if perhaps I *did* have a problem. Why was I afraid of not being clean?

Years back, I had participated in a very powerful seminar that focused on getting in touch with my "real self," and decided to use that process now, to look into the source of my fearful behavior. Once I could identify what my behavior was about, and where it had come from, I would be able to "fix" the problem.

In deep meditation, I regressed to my childhood in Persia. I went back to a day when I was about five years old, joyfully playing in the mud and dirt with some other kids. My wealthy uncle, who was highly respected, was bringing his family to have dinner with us that evening.

When they arrived at our house, my uncle walked to where I was playing with my friends, stared at my muddied feet, and glared at me viciously. Fear and terror suddenly engulfed me. I had goose bumps and was so frightened that I couldn't even cry. In terror I ran into the house, but he followed me, and opened the door to the room where I was hiding. Then he glared at my feet again and called for my mother.

"How can you allow anyone in your family to get so dirty?" he demanded.

Mother smiled and replied, "He is only a child—he enjoys playing in the mud. Do not worry; I'll get him cleaned up."

My uncle gave me a stern look and left the room. "Bijan-jon, let's wash your feet," my mother said with a gentle smile.

I felt comforted by her, but the experience left a very deep impression in my subconscious mind. Unfortunately, Persia only had public baths at that time, so my subconscious desire to be "squeaky clean" would not be able to manifest itself until I reached America, where I might shower as often as I wished.

As I came out of this meditation and realized the source of my "problem," I decided to write to my uncle, who now lived in Tokyo. In detail, I reminded him of the incident and told him about the impact that it had made on me. I also assured him that I had forgiven him. It was only my ego that had kept this fear alive, and the fear didn't really have anything to do with him. I sent the letter without a worry or concern about how he might react; it was something that I had had to do for myself, to complete my process of healing.

The day that I mailed the letter, I felt a wonderful sense of peace. And from that point on, whenever the old fear returned, I would immediately identify it as belonging to my ego, which lived inside of that frightened child. Then I would release the fear, refusing to take part in my ego's story.

Since that experience, I have been at peace with my body, my personal hygiene and myself.

EGO AND THE SNAKE

The snake is a reptile that does what it does. It does not kill for pleasure or for sport, but kills only for food or in fear.

The belief system we have attached to the snake—identifying it as sneaky, cruel, slimy, two-faced and forked-tongued—is truly unjustified. But that belief system perfectly describes ego.

Ego is sneaky, cruel, slimy, two-faced and forked-tongued. It never confronts us head-on, because it knows we would not tolerate its attack; we would abandon it. So instead, ego always waits for an opportunity to sneak in when we least expect it to appear. Then ego brings its darkness upon us and uses us as allies, taking us deep into turmoil, where there is only darkness.

Ego's invasion of our mind is very obvious when we are vigilant for the light and for peace, because ego's purpose is contradictory to that. The more we are vigilant for the light, the easier it becomes to recognize ego's sneaky attacks upon us.

LEARNING THROUGH
JOY AND LAUGHTER

Having lived in many different countries and experienced many different religions, I noticed one thing that the religions had in common: they were all *very* serious. No matter which religion I followed, I always felt humble and small. Every one of them seemed to confirm and solidify this feeling within me.

So when I first established contact with my guides, I was petrified. I thought that I would have to be very serious with them, too. This did not last very long, though, because they were always laughing and joyous.

Then, when my guides first gave me the vision of *Absolutely Effortless Prosperity*, I was told that it would be a tool for learning, based upon joy, laughter and the sharing of miracles. My previous experiences made me wonder, "Could we really learn from joy and laughter?" I decided to ask one of my guides.

"You learn *only* from joy and laughter, and from having fun," he replied. "Being too serious is a reflection of fear—of your unconscious mind's belief in your own sin and guilt. Your thoughts are in the past, rather than in the present."

"To expand your consciousness and to grow, you must be in the joy of the present," he added. "The real masters are always in the present. They know that this world is a game and that we are all meant to have fun and to enjoy it."

Then he went on to tell me about his own life on this planet. While he was in a body, he had been a master. "I was always laughing—I always had a smile on my face," he said. "Everyone around me was aware of my joy. Though some tried to project their own feelings of guilt, sin, and anger onto me, nothing could change my state of mind."

"Bijan," he continued, "When you know who you are and how magnificent you are, you will realize how much you are loved and cared for. All you will want to do is laugh and share your miracles. This is a natural part of your being in a state of peace, which is always available to you. Through *Effortless Prosperity* you will share this knowledge with all of your sisters and brothers. Just remember to have fun!"

UNCONDITIONAL LOVE

From 1982 through 1985, I lived in Australia, where I owned and operated a gym. During those years, my mother lived with me. One particular evening when I returned home from work, I could see that my mother was worried about something. I hugged and kissed her, and asked her what was the matter. She looked at me and said, "I am surprised you have not noticed."

"Noticed what?" I asked.

"Noticed that I am getting fat and that I need to lose some weight," my mother said. "I thought that since you own a gym, you might take me there and train me."

This was very bewildering. I had never been aware of my mother's body before; in fact, I wasn't even conscious that she *had* one. Now I looked at her and gasped. "Oh, no! You *do* have a body—a short, chubby body! I've never noticed it before!" We both had a great laugh over this, and I agreed to begin taking her to the gym.

Within a few minutes I realized that her body had disappeared again. Again, all I could see and feel was my wonderful unconditional love for her, and her unconditional love for me.

I had forgotten about that incident until recently, when my twelve year-old son, Michael, came to visit. While he was staying with me, his mother Kathy called. She asked me if I had noticed how tall Michael had become and how long his legs were. Just as Kathy finished speaking, Michael came out of his bedroom, wearing shorts. I *did* notice how long his legs were—but what *really* surprised me was that he *had* legs!

"Holy cow, Michael, you *do* have legs—and such *long* ones!" I said. He looked at me as if I was crazy, but the truth was that I had never noticed Michael's body before. As with my mother, all that I had ever been aware of was the unconditional love that I felt for this wonderful light in my life.

If I notice a person's body, there is usually some form of judgment attached. And where there is judgment, there cannot be unconditional love or the peace that it brings. When I have unconditional love for someone, I am not aware of his or her body. I only see the light of this perfect child of God.

So now, whenever someone remarks that Michael is getting taller, I have to look away from the love that I have for him, in order to judge whether he truly is taller. Otherwise, he is always simply a bright light of unconditional love that brings joy into my life.

FEELINGS VERSUS EMOTIONS

It is very important for us to distinguish between our feelings and our emotions.

Feelings come from *inside of us*. They bring us into the present, where we can receive the guidance that we need in making decisions. It is here in feelings that our Spirit—the unconditional love that is who we really are—lives. Feelings never waver or change. We always know by our feelings whether something is good for us or not. If it is good for us, we feel peace, and we allow the good to come in. We can always trust our feelings.

Emotions, on the other hand, come from our *ego* and always concern the past or the future. Emotions never have anything to do with our reality. They are constantly changing to reflect what is happening *outside of us*; we can be in peace one moment, then suddenly descend into turmoil the next, with just one wrong word from someone. We can never trust our emotions; when we react from them, turmoil is always the outcome.

Right action comes from our feelings. It is our feelings that tell us what is best for us to do in any situation. When we distinguish between our feelings and our emotions, and choose to follow our feelings, peace is always the result.

YOU ARE EVERYTHING

At the end of one of my seminars in Las Vegas, a good friend of mine named Jack approached me and asked if he could tell me about a problem he was having. He said that during his meditations he always asked his angels for things that he needed, but he had not received anything yet. He asked if I would talk to my guides about this.

When I asked my guides why Jack was having a problem with manifestation, they pointed out that God is like a genie in a bottle. He does not have a point of view and is always ready and willing to manifest wishes, but He does *not* determine *how* you want your wish manifested. He simply gives you what you ask for.

My guides continued, explaining that if Jack says, "I need that," God gives him what he is asking for, which is the experience of *needing that*. But as God gives Jack what he is asking for, which is to need that, He then thinks that Jack does not have what he was asking for—the feeling of need—so God grants him *more need*.

To clear up any confusion I might have on this matter, my guides explained, "You were born with everything; you were created with everything and as everything. Not only do you *have* everything, but more important, you *are* everything. And so, all the experiences that you have, all the things that happen to you, all the incidents that you experience, do not add anything to you or give you anything. They are only experiences and incidents that help to uncover the vision—the knowledge—that you are everything and have everything."

"So with every thought, you go backward or you go forward," my guides said. "You go backward by having more judgement, more evaluation and more cover-ups of the knowledge that you are everything and have everything. You go forward by removing the veil from your eyes, clearing your vision and realizing that you are and have everything."

My guides concluded by saying that in order for us to discover how powerful we are, first we have to get in touch with the reality, which is that we are everything and we have everything. "The Father did not hold back on anything," they said. "The Father gave us everything, and created us as everything. When we get in touch with this truth, we realize that all we have to do is remove the veil and simply enjoy life, in total peace at every moment."

After talking with my guides I understood that there is nothing for me to want or need. Everything is already here for me.

LETTING GO OF THE PAST

My brother John called me one day to express his gratitude for the copy of *Absolutely Effortless Prosperity* I had sent him. He said that he had been studying it faithfully and that it had changed his life. Then, before our conversation ended, he told me he would like some advice from my guide and me.

He said he was interviewing people to fill a key position in his company, and had found someone who was very well qualified. There was only one problem—he was unable to reach any of the candidate's previous employers, so he might verify the man's credentials.

My brother explained that the last time he had hired someone under the same conditions, the employee had taken advantage of him by sneaking a lot of money and business from the company when he left. So now John was torn between his desire to hire this highly qualified candidate, and a reluctance about hiring him based on the previous bad experience.

I said that I would speak with my guide and call back as soon as I had some information.

The next morning during my meditation, I talked to my guide about John's dilemma. My guide listened patiently and then spoke.

116

"Your brother has a dilemma because he is not in the present," he said. "John is judging this man by past experiences, and doing this never serves anyone well. All of your brother's fear comes from the past; if he were in the present, he would accept this man as a magnificent addition to his company."

That was all I needed to know. Right after my meditation, I called John and asked him to explain, once again, why he felt so uncomfortable about hiring this man. He answered easily, "Because of my past experience."

"And what if you had not had that past experience?" I asked. "Deep in your heart, how do you feel about this man?"

"You know, Bijan-jon," he said, "I feel total peace about him. I trust him, and I *do* want him in my company. He is exactly the man I am looking for. The only thing that brings up fear is my past experience."

Before I could say anything else, my brother began to laugh. "I get it, I get it," he said. "You are always telling me that all fear and guilt come from the past—that the guilt of the past determines the fear of the future. I guess I am afraid that, in the future, he might hurt me. But the truth is that he won't."

"That is up to you,' I said. "A moment ago you told me that deep within your heart is a feeling of peace about this man. If you have gone within, to where unconditional love is, and you have found peace, then peace is what you will have."

As our conversation ended, I understood that the lesson was more for me than it was for John. Often, because of some past experience, I have gone against choices that have felt comfortable and peaceful to me. Realizing this, I knew I would no longer allow the past to determine what choices I might make. Instead, I would go to where unconditional love was, within me, to find the answer there.

Since then, every choice I have made has been perfect, and my life has been much happier.

IF ONLY I COULD HAVE

One morning, as I was working out and laughing with my good friend Danny, he pointed to the far side of the gym and said, "Now *that* is the kind of girl I really like! If I could be with her, I would never ask for anything else."

I looked in the direction he was pointing. A good-looking blond girl was walking toward us, and I recognize her immediately. It was Penny, the former girlfriend of a bodybuilder friend of mine. I waved at her and she came over to say hello, which gave me the opportunity to introduce her to Danny. They hit it off very quickly and after awhile they left the gym together.

I did not see or talk to Danny for a couple of weeks. Then one day as I was working out alone, I saw Danny and Penny walking in. I was looking forward to hearing the love story that had begun two weeks ago, and I watched as Penny waved and walked to the Stairmaster, while Danny walked straight to me.

After the normal greeting and some small talk, I asked, "Now that your wishes have come true, how are you feeling?"

He gave me a smile, shook his head and said, "I have one more wish." Then he looked over at Penny on the Stairmaster and said, "Now if only I could get rid of her." I laughed, but he stopped me and said, "Bijan, she doesn't leave me alone for a moment. I can't breathe. If only I could get rid of her, I would never ask for any thing else." Then he got quiet for a moment and asked, "What do you think my lesson is in this matter, Mr. Excellent?"

I told him that whenever I ask for what I desire, I always say, "Please give it to me only if it is good for me and will bring me joy. Otherwise, do not give it to me, no matter how much I ask for it."

"Through experience I have found out that not every thing I ask for is good for me or brings me peace and joy," I explained to him. "In this case, you did not put the disclaimer behind your wishes, so you got what you asked for even though it did not bring you peace and joy."

He smiled and said, "I promises you, Mr. Excellent, that it will not happen again."

DIRECTIONS IN LIFE

In my dream, I had just boarded a train bound for New York. I found a window seat and settled in, looking forward to the scenic experience of the trip.

While waiting for the train to leave the station, I started listening to the people around me. They were talking about how much better Florida is than New York this time of the year. I had already chosen to go to New York, but now my ego said, "Go to Florida!" The more I listened to the people talking about Florida, the more my ego told me I should be going there—and the more unhappy I became. I was in turmoil. "Why is this train going to New York?" I thought.

Finally the train left the station; as it gained speed, my ego gained power. "Change the direction of the train!" I yelled. I even tried to change the train's direction myself. But no matter how much turmoil my ego created, the train kept following its track.

We passed magnificent countryside along the way, but my ego was so powerful that I did not even notice. Throughout the entire trip and at every stop, my ego and the egos of the other passengers just kept talking about how horrible it was going to be in New York, and how wonderful it would be if the train were going to Florida.

Finally we ended up in New York. From the first moment I had boarded, to the last stop before we arrived, there had been many opportunities for me to change trains and go in a different direction. But I had given control to ego.

And ego had been so busy throwing a fit about going somewhere that other people said was not good, that it had even caused me to miss what I had been so looking forward to: the scenic experience of the trip.

EVERYONE IS IN HIS
PERFECT PLACE

While driving to California with my son Michael one day, I noticed he was not in a very good mood. My first thought was that I should try to pull him out of it—I could tell jokes or start a conversation about something I knew he was interested in.

Then I remembered that these attempts had never helped in the past. In fact, they had always seemed to keep him in his bad mood for a longer time than if I had just ignored his mood and let him be.

So, because I love him unconditionally, I decided to respect and honor his choice to be wherever he was. This would allow him to have the experience he had created for himself.

This led to a realization: if I felt unconditional love for everyone, I would respect and honor everyone as well. In the past, I had always thought that if I was happy, then everyone should be happy; if I was upset, then everyone should be upset. But if I respected others the way I respect Michael, then I would also respect the choices they made for themselves. If they chose to be happy, angry or disappointed, that was up to them. To me, they would always be perfect children of God, in their perfect places, no matter where that might be.

The interesting lesson for me was that after a few minutes of allowing my son to be where he was, he suddenly changed his mood. He said, "Dad, let's tell some jokes and laugh. I don't like to be unhappy—let's have some fun!"

It seems that whenever I simply give up control in a situation, it always works out the way that is best for me.

CREATING FROM
CONSCIOUS THOUGHT

At every moment, our thoughts are creating our world. Everything that we see outside of us is the result of our thinking made manifest in form and matter. Because there are no idle thoughts, every thought that we have is creating either a positive or a negative experience in our lives.

When I first became aware of my thoughts, I began to notice that I often create some that are totally unnecessary—just to create. For instance, I noticed that whenever I am in a hurry while driving, the cars in front of me move out of my way, so that I have a clear road ahead and can do the maximum speed limit. But then, when I finally arrive at my destination, I am always early.

What I ultimately realized from having this happen again and again, was that I would have been on time even if I had not had a clear road! Without being aware of it, I was creating unnecessarily.

How I create unnecessarily became very obvious to me after an experience that I had one day at the gym. Whenever I need to park in a public place, I always create a space that is very close to the entrance, so I don't have to walk very far. And as I drove into the parking lot on this particular morning,

I created a parking space right next to the door. Happily I parked the car, entered the gym, went straight to the treadmill—and *walked for five miles.*

At the time, I was not even conscious of what I had done, or of the significance of it. But as I thought about the situation later, I couldn't help but laugh at myself.

Sometimes what I create is unnecessary, and it must be that I do it just to remind myself that I am the Creator. So, it is important that I become aware of my thoughts, in order to create consciously rather than unconsciously.

THE RIGHT CHOICE

Whenever we are faced with several choices, it is always one choice that is truth—the right choice. The rest are ego's choices, and we all know that ego tries to confuse us with many, many choices.

When we make the right choice, there is no lesson involved; instead, there is just peace, love and joy. But when we make the wrong choice, the universe readjusts itself, coming into alignment with our choice.

The time between the moment when we make a wrong choice and the moment when the universe has shifted into alignment with it, is the time when we learn our lesson. It is a time when we learn that if we had made the right choice, there would have been no lesson to learn.

So we make the right choice because we are children of God, the Creator, the Power Source. And when we make the wrong choice, God's love guides us through our lesson, to bring us closer to Him.

WHERE DO WE GO AFTER THE BODY

There are a lot of old and fearful belief systems regarding where we go after the body, and because you are very powerful, a belief in any one of them will manifest it as your reality. But reality is not always truth, and in order to know the *truth* of where we go after the body, you must *release* the old belief systems. Holding on to an old belief system which has fear in it is like looking through a colored glass to see everything. The truth that comes from God is not colored with any fear or condemnation—it is simply the pure light of all unconditional love, all power and all joy.

Where *do* we go after the body? When you leave your body, for whatever reason, it does not *feel* like you left it. You are still "there", but you are just not surrounded by the body anymore. You feel free and unlimited.

It is hard to imagine those feelings as long as you are in this limited body. You can be anywhere that you desire, just by thinking it, and you can be more than one place at the same time. Your vibration is so fast and high that no one in the physical body can see or hear you—but you can see and hear them all.

You realize that all your challenges, worries and cares were only about the body which you are not concerned about any more. You know that everyone is on the right path, learning what he or she has chosen to learn, and you don't have to do anything or be concerned about any one of them.

The last thing that you will notice before leaving to go to the higher realm of consciousness is that we all have so many guides and angels to show us the right path that we are all safe and sound. That is the moment when you will look up and remember who you are, and understand that it is up to you whether you stay on this planet or go to different dimensions and different universes. It is all up to you. Whatever you wish to experience at that moment, you choose.

My job is to tell you about what you will ultimately know anyway—to tell you what will take the fear away. The experiences out there, without the body, are not better or worse; they are just *different*. This book is not about limiting you and putting the fear in you so you become dependent upon me, or upon other people. This book is about reminding you of the truth—that you are the child of God and you create your own reality.

Enjoy having the body as long as you wish, and then release it without fear, so you may enjoy experiences without the body.

ONENESS

A lot of time we think that oneness is reached by dying and leaving the body. Dying does not lead to oneness: the truth is that oneness is always reached by *living without separation.*

What puts a separation between everyone and me is my judgment, evaluation, and dark thoughts. I am very clear when I don't have any dark thoughts at all—when the only thought that I do have is the thought of oneness with everyone else and with the Father. This creates the state of joy, peace and love.

As we come into this world, before we develop ego, we have no thought of separation; in truth, we have no private or individual thoughts at all. To us, everything is simply about love, and so we feel the oneness of it; everything belongs to us as we belong to everything. That is why, as children, we like to share everything we have and to have everyone else share with us. We feel no separation.

Then as ego appears, we accumulate more and more dark thoughts. They become like a wall that cuts us off from the rest of the world and makes us individuals with a point of view, judgement, and evaluation. Once we let go of ego and bring down the wall of separation, what we see is only the truth. We see that we are part of the whole universe, and all that can show up is joy, peace and love. All of our other parts support this part of us, so we can be joyous. There is no jealousy, grievance or anger.

If I put that wall of separation around me, the fear grows to be enormous, because now I am this small being with a wall around me, up against the whole universe. The fear and the wall do not disappear by giving up or by dying. They disappear when we let go of ego and release dark thoughts of grievances, jealousy and resentment.

So, the more I laugh and shine light into my dark thoughts, the more that the wall disappears—and the more I become aware of my oneness with everyone else and with the Father.

Remember that all power, strength, and joy come from the oneness— from knowing that we are one with everyone and everything. That is the only way for us to create and manifest wonderful things for ourselves. Remember the knowledge, and know that God created you to be like Himself.

This process does not take any effort. You simply must be willing to remember yourself. At the moment when you open up to willingness, all the action and doing happens in such a way that it is totally effortless.

ACE IN THE HOLE

It was my fiance Samia's, birthday. I wished that it would be a special day for her, so I sent her some flowers at work, and then when she got home I asked her where she would like to have her birthday dinner. She said her favorite restaurant was Buzio's, at the Rio Hotel. So, Samia, my son Michael and I drove to the Rio.

When we arrived at Buzio's there was a short wait for a table. I asked Samia to stay in line for a few moments while Michael and I checked something out; I was hoping to surprise her with tickets to see the Danny Gans show. These tickets were known to be sold-out for a month in advance, but I thought I would check it out anyway.

Michael and I went to the pit boss, and I asked him if he could help me get tickets. Laughing, he told me that would be impossible—but then he suggested that I check with the VIP room.

When we got to the VIP room, the young lady there told me that Danny Gans tickets were sold out a month in advance, and tonight they would be especially impossible to get, since the rodeo was in town. Michael suggested we forget about getting any tickets and just enjoy Samia's birthday dinner, but I told him that I still had an ace in the hole.

Michael asked what it was, and I said, "God." Then I closed my eyes for a moment and prayed.

When I finished my prayer, we walked to the ticket booth. I handed my credit card to the man behind the window and asked him for three tickets to see the Danny Gans show. He asked me if we had reservations, and I replied, "No." He laughed and told me everything was sold out.

Then as he glanced at his computer screen, his eyes opened wide in amazement. "What did you do?" he asked. "How can this be? This has never happened before!" When Michael asked the man what had happened, he looked up from his computer screen and said, "Four tickets in the very first row, center-stage were just cancelled." He quickly told the other agents that three of these tickets were sold. I smiled because I knew what was happening.

Michael looked at me and said, "You did it!"

"No, Michael, I did not do it—but my *angel* did," I answered. "My angel is such a show off!" We laughed together and walked back to the restaurant with our surprise for Samia, knowing that we had just witnessed a great miracle.

GLOSSARY

*Be
vigilant
for the light.*

GLOSSARY

Effortless Prosperity is about *being* in the present. In the present moment, we are totally provided for as precious children of God. We need not *do* anything that comes from ego in order to be effortlessly prosperous; miracles simply show up constantly and effortlessly. We become the creators of our universe, manifesting everything we ask for. To have effortless prosperity is to be in total peace.

Ego is the part of the mind that miscreates. Ego loves darkness and turmoil, and it loves *stories* about darkness and turmoil. It lives in the *guilt* of the past and in the *fear* of the future. Ego blocks and denies our ability to bring forth our inheritance from our Creator; through its denial of our inner goodness, it undermines our attempts to grow to higher levels. Ego speaks to us in the languages of criticism, judgment, insecurity, scarcity, separation, sacrifice and fear. When we listen to ego, turmoil is always the result.

Extension is the way in which God creates. He extended Himself and created us. When we share our love, we are extending as God does.

Function is our mission while we are here on Earth. Our function is to heal ourselves and others through love and forgiveness.

Healing is our function; it is what occurs when our minds join with the minds of our sisters and brothers, to experience wholeness. When we join in healing, we release our illusions of guilt and sin, and replace them with joy and peace.

Joy is the door we walk through, to reach peace.

Judgment is our distorted opinion. It is our ego's mistaken belief that we have all of the facts that are necessary for evaluating and discerning. When we judge others, we are really judging ourselves.

Light (spiritual light) is anything which brings joy, peace, love, healing and deeper spirituality. It is the Divine Presence in each of us.

Miracle is a shift in perception. It is the natural state of things when the flow of life is unobstructed. Miracles occur when, through the help of Spirit, we offer a sister or brother forgiveness and love instead of judgment and attack. Miracles create healing, and healing releases us from guilt, fear and anger. Miracles are not sized.

Peace is a sense of well-being and calmness that allows light to flow through us, and allows miracles to be recognized more easily. It occurs when we are in the present moment rather than in the past or future. Peace is our ultimate goal. We acquire it through healing, by forgiving and loving.

Perception is our interpretation of the world we live in. It is distorted by ego, and is always changing because it is based on the ego's judgments. *See also Shift in perception.*

Projection is the process by which we get rid of our guilt, fear and anger by thrusting them onto someone or something else. What we see outside of ourselves is simply a reflection of what we see inside of ourselves.

Prosperity is not simply about having financial abundance. it is about having excellent health and joyful relationships. Without all of these things, we cannot be in peace. When we are in peace, we have prosperity in *every* area of our lives.

Shift in perception is when we choose to see differently. Instead of listening to our ego, which brings up fear and guilt, we listen to Holy Spirit and extend the love of God, which brings us peace. A shift in perception is a miracle.

Spirit is often referred to as Holy Spirit. Spirit speaks to us in the languages of love, truth, joy and faith; it is our oneness with God. When we follow Spirit's guidance, we experience joy, peace, abundance and growth.

Story always talks about the *past*. A story is never about the present moment. Often, ego will add drama and exaggeration to a story, for more effect. When a story is used to preface a miracle, it brings turmoil to the speaker and to the listener.

Vigilant for the light means that we constantly monitor our thoughts, and what we see, hear and say. Remember that we are not here to monitor others; we are here to be vigilant for the light in *ourselves* and in our *interactions* with others. Vigilance requires that we consciously choose only thoughts, conversations, activities and relationships that will keep us in the light. Vigilant is not about *doing*; vigilant is about *being*—being *steadfast*.

MIRACLE
JOURNAL

*Miracles
are like little children.
The more you notice them,
the more they come out and play.*

Notice your miracles!

SPIRIT SPEAKS THROUGH ME

At every event, just say, "This is here only to bless me."

DAY 2 ~ LESSON 32
I LISTEN ONLY TO WHAT BRINGS ME JOY

At every event, just say, "This is here only to bless me."

DAY 3 ~ LESSON 33
I SEE THE LIGHT IN MYSELF AND OTHERS

At every event, just say, "This is here only to bless me."

I AM OPEN TO KNOW
THE REAL MEANING OF WHAT I SEE

At every event, just say, "This is here only to bless me."

DAY 5 ~ LESSON 35
THE LIGHT IS ALWAYS HERE

At every event, just say, "This is here only to bless me."

I AM THE LIGHT

DAY 7 ~ LESSON 37
I AM PROSPEROUS IN ALL ASPECTS
OF MY LIFE

At every event, just say, "This is here only to bless me."

I AM WHOLE AND COMPLETE

At every event, just say, "This is here only to bless me."

EVERYONE DESERVES
EFFORTLESS PROSPERITY

At every event, just say, "This is here only to bless me."

I AM RECEIVING ALL OF GOD'S GIFTS

At every event, just say, "This is here only to bless me."

I GIVE JUST BECAUSE I HAVE

At every event, just say, "This is here only to bless me."

LOVE IS MY REALITY

At every event, just say, "This is here only to bless me."

MY MIND IS IN TOTAL PEACE

At every event, just say, "This is here only to bless me."

**ONLY WHAT IS BEST FOR ME
SHOWS UP IN MY LIFE**

At every event, just say, "This is here only to bless me."

DAY 15 ~ LESSON 45
I AM ETERNAL

At every event, just say, "This is here only to bless me."

MY THOUGHTS FLOW
FROM MY LOVING FATHER

MY LIFE IS FULL OF MIRACLES

At every event, just say, "This is here only to bless me."

DAY 18 ~ LESSON 48
I AM PEACEFUL

At every event, just say, "This is here only to bless me."

160

I AM A LOVING AND LOVABLE
CHILD OF GOD

At every event, just say, "This is here only to bless me."

FEAR DOES NOT EXIST

At every event, just say, "This is here only to bless me."

DAY 21 ~ LESSON 51
I AM THE LOVE OF GOD

At every event, just say, "This is here only to bless me."

163

I AM SURROUNDED BY UNCONDITIONAL LOVE

At every event, just say, "This is here only to bless me."

GOD TRUSTS ME COMPLETELY

At every event, just say, "This is here only to bless me."

MY SOURCE AND I ARE ONE

At every event, just say, "This is here only to bless me."

I AM GRATEFUL
THAT GOD IS IN CONTROL

At every event, just say, "This is here only to bless me."

DAY 26 ~ LESSON 56
I AM BLESSED AT THE CREATOR
OF MY WORLD

At every event, just say, "This is here only to bless me."

DAY 27 ~ LESSON 57
THE WILL OF GOD IS MY WILL

At every event, just say, "This is here only to bless me."
169

DAY 28 ~ LESSON 58
I SEE UNCONDITIONAL LOVE
EVERYWHERE

At every event, just say, "This is here only to bless me."

I ACKNOWLEDGE MY HIGHER SELF

At every event, just say, "This is here only to bless me."

I AM CONSTANTLY COMMUNICATING
WITH UNCONDITIONAL LOVE

At every event, just say, "This is here only to bless me."

EFFORTLESS CATALOG

Give yourself and others
the gift
of
Effortless Prosperity
books, tapes and CD's

by
Bijan

Note:
This catalog is current as of March 2001.
Please call or check the website for new product listings.

LET THE MIRACLES BEGIN!

ABSOLUTELY EFFORTLESS PROSPERITY, BOOK I
ISBN 1-930455-00-3 *212 pages* $15.00/ea.

Why not have everything you desire? No one deserves it more! This book contains 30 simple yet profound lessons that will lead you out of a world of darkness and limitation into a world of light, abundance, and unlimited possibilities. Take the journey into spiritual awareness with these lessons that Bijan has received from Spirit. Learn the secret behind the misperception of cause and effect. Know that the power of creation exists within you, in your ability to choose and direct your thoughts and emotions. This book can transform your life in 30 days.

BOOK I –FARSI TRANSLATION $12.00/ea.
PROSPERITY AFFIRMATIONS IN FARSI $10.00/ea.

ABSOLUTELY EFFORTLESS PROSPERITY, BOOK I 16-TAPE SET
ISBN 1-930455-07-0 *16 tapes-30 minutes/side* $75.00/set

Let Bijan be your personal guide, taking you on your journey into spiritual awareness! This companion tape set for *Absolutely Effortless Prosperity Book I* consists of the 30 daily lessons on 15 tapes, plus Bijan's *Keep Your Word* tape. Perfect for individual use and with Effortless Prosperity Study Groups.

BOOKMARK – 30 LESSONS
ABSOLUTELY EFFORTLESS PROSPERITY, BOOK I
BMK1 $1.00/ea.
BMK1 Special   12/$10.00

"Bijan's work beautifully complements the technologies that we teach...I've recommended it to many of my students who have also achieved outstanding results. Thank-you!"
Bob Quintana, President, Anthony Robbins & Associates
The Unlimited Success Group, Inc.

Prices do not include shipping and handling charges
Please call or write for study group volume discounts.

THE JOURNEY CONTINUES!

ABSOLUTELY EFFORTLESS PROSPERITY, BOOK II
ISBN 1-930455-50-X *208 pages* $15.00/ea.

In the thirty lessons of *Absolutely Effortless Prosperity Book I*, Bijan guided you from the realm of doing into the realm of being. Now, continue your journey with advanced lessons that take you even deeper into this level of consciousness. As being becomes more familiar, you will truly understand that—at every moment—you can create all that you desire, with complete joy and peace.

Book II's thirty daily lessons will guide you toward:

Learning - what the Black Hole is, and how to cover it up
Recognizing - and letting go of self-limiting belief systems
Knowing - the one simple truth in every event
Seeing - all the miracles in your daily life
Receiving - the joyful abundance the Universe has to offer

Revised and expanded for 2001, *Absolutely Effortless Prosperity, Book II* has a glossary of terms and a 30-day journal for recording miracles.

ABSOLUTELY EFFORTLESS PROSPERITY, BOOK II 16-TAPE SET
ISBN 1-930455-08-9 *16 tapes-30 minutes/side* $75.00/set

Continue your journey with Bijan, as he personally guides you to an even deeper level of experience. This companion tape set for *Absolutely Effortless Prosperity Book II* consists of lessons 31-60 on 15 tapes, plus Bijan's *This Is Here Only To Bless Me* tape. A must-have for personal use and with Effortless Prosperity Study Groups.

> *"I used to believe most of the things Bijan taught—*
> *and now I believe everything he teaches!*
> *The reason? My ratings are the highest they have ever been,*
> *because I stay totally in the light."*
> Joey Reynolds
> WOR Radio, New York

Prices do not include shipping and handling charges
Please call or write for study group volume discounts.

HOW TO BE OPEN TO RECEIVE
VOLUME I
4-TAPE SET

ISBN 1-930455-09-7 $35.00/set

SEMINAR I
EFFORTLESS PROSPERITY BASICS

It is so easy to allow the miracles and wonderful things to flow in when we know the basics of Effortless Prosperity and this magnificent Universe. *90 minutes*

SEMINAR II
GOD IS JOY

Down deep, we all want to be close to Spirit. Unless we know and are very clear that Spirit is joy, and that Spirit wants us to have joy, we feel that suffering is what will get us closer to Spirit. *90 minutes*

SEMINAR III
YOU ARE WORTHY AND DESERVING

We all deserve to have prosperity that is flowing very effortlessly, relationships that are joyous and health that is flawless. If you do not feel worthy and deserving on some level, then you need to listen to this tape. *90 minutes*

SEMINAR IV
NOTICING AND RELINQUISHING
YOUR LIMITATION

Limitations are what keep us unhappy. As you listen to this tape and begin to let go of your limitations, you will realize what a powerful, creative, unlimited spirit you are. Soon your life will be joyous. *60 minutes*

SEMINAR TAPES SOLD INDIVIDUALLY @ $10.00/each
Seminar I: ISBN 1-930455-24-0
Seminar II: ISBN 1-930455-25-9
Seminar III: ISBN 1-930455-26-7
Seminar IV: ISBN 1-930455-27-5

Prices do not include shipping and handling charges.
Please call or write for study group volume discounts

177

HOW TO BE OPEN TO RECEIVE
VOLUME II
4-TAPE SET

ISBN 1-930455-10-0 $35.00/set

SEMINAR V
RECLAIM YOUR POWERS
BY GIVING UP JUDGMENT

Judgment is like a blanket covering up our powers. As you listen more and more to this tape, slowly but surely you will give up your judgments and reclaim your unlimited powers. *60 minutes*

SEMINAR VI
RELINQUISHING OLD BELIEF SYSTEMS

Our belief systems literally create our world outside of us. This tape gets you in tune with those inherited belief systems that do not work in your life. It will show you an easy way to correct them and have new choices in your life. *60 minutes*

SEMINAR VII
LET GO OF SACRIFICES

This tape will get you in touch with the belief in sacrifice, which is manifesting from your unconscious mind. It will show you the simple way to release sacrifice, so you can be back in your Spirit-given right of joy. *60 minutes*

SEMINAR VIII
RECOVER YOUR KINGDOM

When you **know** that heaven is where you are now and that you have only this moment, you will manifest the truth and your life will become joyous, effortless and free. This tape will get you in touch with that truth. *60 minutes*

SEMINAR TAPES SOLD INDIVIDUALLY @ $10.00/each
Seminar V: ISBN 1-930455-28-3
Seminar VI: ISBN 1-930455-29-1
Seminar VII: ISBN 1-930455-30-5
Seminar VIII: ISBN 1-930455-31-3

Prices do not include shipping and handling charges.
Please call or write for study group volume discounts

EFFORTLESS HEALTH—ABSOLUTELY!

THE COMMON SENSE
OF EFFORTLESS HEALTH - The Book
ISBN 1-930455-12-7 *112 pages* $10.00/ea.
In this book, Bijan—Mr. Universe 1993 and 1994 Natural Division—
explains how you can be totally healthy and how to look and feel good
effortlessly. With nutritional guidance and simple exercises, you will see
how much fun life can be.

EFFORTLESS HEALTH - The Tape
ISBN 1-930455-11-9 *60 minutes.* $10.00/ea.
On this tape, Bijan—a former Mr. Universe-Natural Division—shares his
knowledge of how to have effortless health through nutrition and peace
of mind, bringing your immune system into balance.

AFFIRMATIONS & MEDITATIONS

EFFORTLESS PROSPERITY LAUGHTER
WITH SUBLIMINAL AFFIRMATIONS
ISBN 1-930455-13-5 *30minutes* $10.00/ea.
Laughter is opening to receive joy. With the addition of subliminal
affirmations, this tape is an effortless way to open your mind to receiving
prosperity and abundance. A must in every car or Walkman.

EFFORTLESS PROSPERITY AFFIRMATIONS
FOR EVERYONE
ISBN 1-930455-14-3 *60 minutes* $10.00/ea.
This tape is a must for every household. Bijan's very simple affirmations
can bring you, your family, and all your loved ones to the state of being
open to receive by knowing that you are worthy and deserving NOW!
(—not after suffering or doing anything). Leave this tape on auto reverse
and don't take it off until you see the results in yourself and in the ones
around you.

MEDITATION
ISBN 1-930455-15-1 *30 minutes* $ 8.00/ea.
This meditation by Bijan will bring you to a peaceful healing place where
you can find quietness of mind, so you will discover who you really are.

Prices do not include shipping and handling charges.
Please call or write for study group volume discounts.

—AND MORE!

HAVING AN EFFORTLESS AND JOYOUS JOB
ISBN 1/930455-16-X *60 minutes* $10.00/ea.
You have to imagine the change in your attitude and in your productivity when you truly love and enjoy your job. This simple yet profound tape will get you in touch with that great joy—and eventually you will want all your loved ones to hear this tape.

GIVING & RECEIVING
ISBN 1-930455-17-8 *60 minutes* $10.00/ea.
This tape shows you step by step how to open yourself to receive all the gifts of the Universe—effortlessly. You will get in touch with how to open more to receive, and you will in turn become more giving, thus realizing that giving and receiving are one and the same.

ATTAIN MASTERY
ISBN 1-930455-18-6 *60 minutes* $10.00/ea.
This is very high-quality information which gets one in touch with the incredible powers that we have inside. We can then operate our lives from the realm of Mastery and Unconditional Love—for ourselves as well as for others.

MANIFESTING CONSCIOUSLY
ISBN 1-930455-36-4 Tape $10.00/ea.
ISBN 1-930455-37-2 CD $15.00/ea.
People on this planet seem to want to DO something to change circumstances, things or events they do not like, forgetting that once the circumstances or events are here, it's already too late. In this profound seminar tape, Bijan will show you how flexible energy is in the now moment, and will teach you how to use energy to manifest only those circumstances and events that you truly desire.

HEALING IN THE NEW MILLENNIUM
ISBN 1-930455-38-0 Tape $10.00/ea.
ISBN 1-930455-39-9 CD $15.00/ea.
This seminar tape will teach you how to heal your body, your circumstances, and ultimately your mind from the effects of events and situations that you no longer desire—and how to heal others in such a way that gets them in touch with their own magnificent powers. Included are powerful exercises that will assist you in releasing and letting go of beliefs in pain, aches, suffering and dis-ease.

EFFORTLESS PROSPERITY FOR CHILDREN (Ages 2-7)

LITTLE FRIENDS OF NATURE, Book I
ISBN 1-930455-04-6 *146 pages* $10.00/ea.
Each of the stories in the children's books not only supports and confirms the thirty lessons of *Effortless Prosperity Books I and II*, but also follows the daily lessons in the same order. Now the entire family can practice the lessons together. Your children will learn to connect with their inner guidance, experience total peace, and increase their sense of self-worth. As they recognize the miracles that occur daily in their lives, their behavior will improve and they will become more loving and joyous. Communication and understanding between you and your children will flow effortlessly.

LITTLE FRIENDS OF NATURE, Book II
ISBN1-930455-21-6 *168pages* $10.00/ea.
The adventures of Jennifer and Melinda continue. *Check for availability.*

EFFORTLESS PROSPERITY FOR YOUTHS (Ages 8-12)

MY GUIDING SPIRIT, Book I
ISBN 1-930455-05-4 *84 pages* $10.00/ea.
Jason and Gabriel, two special brothers, bring the stories and lessons of *Effortless Prosperity* to life through their adventures together.

MY GUIDING SPIRIT, Book II
ISBN 1-930455-22-4 $10.00/ea.
Check for availability.

"Your stories made me listen to my guidance" - Lauren

"I like all the stories because they teach me lots of good stuff." - Katie

""This is the best book I ever read!" - Heather

Prices do not include shipping and handling charges.
Please call or write for study group volume discounts.

EFFORTLESS PROSPERITY FOR
TEENAGERS (Ages 13-18)

LIGHT FROM THE SKY, Book I

ISBN1-930455-01-1 *196 pages* $10.00/ea.

This book is full of interesting and funny stories that follow the thirty-day *Effortless Prosperity* program. Siavash is an adventurous being from another star system whose mission on Earth as a teenager named John is to bring light to as many people as he can, by helping them to let go of fear and get in touch with their creative power. In the most subtle way, it will introduce your teen to the hazards of alcohol and drug use, as well as of negative and unhealthy associations. It is a ***must*** for every teenager.

LIGHT FROM THE SKY, Book II

ISBN 1-930455-23-2 *176 pages* $10.00/ea.

The journey continues with another thirty stories of the light-minded being from another star system, who is visiting Earth to bring the planet back to its natural state of joy, peace, love and effortless prosperity. As with the first book in the series, the volume is based on the lessons of *Absolutely Effortless Prosperity, Book I. Check for availability.*

---

*"During a test at school, I remembered what John in Light From The Sky
had said about letting go of my worries and trusting.
So I did, and answered everything right!"*
- Mike, 14 years old

*"Three days after reading Light From The Sky,
a boy at school wiped his dirty hands on my clean clothes.
Instead of fighting with him, I let it go and walked away."*
- Dominic, 15 years old

*"Bijan's teachings of Effortless Prosperity For Teenagers
have helped me to be more focused in school.
They have also brought my family and me closer together."*
- Steven, 15 years old

*"Ever since I began doing the lessons of Effortless Prosperity,
my mother and I communicate much better with each other,
and she is much more forgiving than she ever was."*
- Michael, 16 years old

Prices do not include shipping and handling charges.
Please call or write for study group volume discounts

ADVANCED MEDITATION
MESSAGE FROM BIJAN

Every time, before I leave on my journey to do astral traveling, Samia hugs me and asks me to promise and to give my word that I will come back. However, when I am out there doing astral traveling, a sense of peace and ecstasy that is not available anywhere on this planet comes over me. To describe it in a poor way in our limited language, it is a sense of being everywhere, totally aware of everything, yet not losing my identity as Bijan.

That is the time when I look, and realize a piece of me is missing. And when I look carefully, I see that the missing piece of me is an awareness that most of my brothers and sisters on this planet still believe in limitation (their bodies, their prosperity and abundance, their relationships, health and language—and most importantly, their unconditional love). ALWAYS at that moment I her the voice of the great Archangel reminding me that I have been in the realm of astral travel many times, and the reason I MUST go back is to bring awareness and remembrance of how magnificent, powerful and unlimited all my brothers and sisters are. That, and the fact that I have given my word to Samia, are the only reasons why I come back every time.

Whenever I return, there is a sense of deep peace and understanding. There is a renewed clarity regarding my function on this planet, which has once again been revealed to me in such a way that I cannot help laughing and being joyful for hours afterward.

If you are reading this, my brothers and sisters, please open yourself to remembering how wonderful, how magnificent, how powerful, how loving and lovable you are. You have no real enemy on this planet. Everyone is here to contribute to you and to your growth—and down deep inside, deeper than being conscious of, everyone loves you so incredibly that they will *act* as your enemy if it will serve you in awakening you to become conscious of your magnificence and power.

I invite you to take this journey with me—and with those of your brothers and sisters who are now open to receive. My function and deepest joy for you is that you become "healed healers" in this new Millennium.

I love you.

Bijan—January 2001

ADVANCED MEDITATION
ABOUT THE TAPES

After the very powerful *Effortless Prosperity Week in Hawaii* **in September 2000,** I was approached by people from all walks of life who suggested that I create a tape set of thirty meditations for the thirty lessons of *Effortless Prosperity Book I.* I asked my guides about it, and they said, "Yes, we must do that—but you have to release the outcome, because we have a higher purpose." I surrendered to the will of my guides and, as you will notice, the result is totally different, and of a much higher quality and vibration than I ever dreamed about.

Spirit delivered these meditations through me, and more than the meaning of what I say in each tape, is the *vibration of my voice and where I come from* which will affect *your* vibration and bring you to a state of peace and joy. The principle of the tuning fork is very powerful, and it is very obvious in these tapes. If you have two tuning forks the same size, and you hide one somewhere and then vibrate the other one, the hidden tuning fork will vibrate at the same frequency as the one you caused to vibrate, because they both have the same cause, form, foundation and spirit. This is the way it is. In like manner, hearing the vibration of my voice, which comes directly from my *spirit*, will reveal to you the unlimited nature of *your* spirit after each meditation.

Our soul is like a tuning fork, and as our beliefs in darkness and limitation, hang-ups and barriers have accumulated over time, a blanket of limitation has covered it in such a way that it no longer vibrates. These meditation tapes vibrate in a full frequency of *limitlessness*, and will bring your soul's tuning fork to the same vibration. Once one tuning fork vibrates at a certain frequency, the other instantly vibrates at that same frequency. As with a tuning fork, once my vibration gets going, it changes the energy and vibration of whoever is in its presence.

To put it another way, these meditation tapes are not so much about what words you will hear, but rather, they are about the vibration of TRUTH FROM SPIRIT. Once we tell the truth, others feel it. It doesn't matter what form or what language we speak, for TRUTH is as powerful as the vibration of the tuning fork.

So do not analyze what I am saying in each tape. Simply be open to receive the vibration.

ADVANCED MEDITATION
A JOURNEY FROM BODY TO SPIRIT

VOLUME I   RELEASING AND CLEARING LIMITATION

ISBN 1-930455-32-1 $75/set

You cannot put water in a full cup—you must empty your mind of limitation before you can fill it with light and remembrances of who you really are. Be comfortable and at peace with Volume I before beginning Volume II.

Tape 1
Side A—Meditation 1 Creating Your "Peace Room"
Side B—Meditation 2 Creating a "Light" to Help You

Tape 2
Side A—Meditation 3 Finding Your Guides and Angels
Side B—Meditation 4 Finding Your Guides at a Deeper Level

Tape 3
Side A—Meditation 5 Tapping the Energy of Gifts of God
Side B—Meditation 6   Healing Relationships

Tape 4
Side A—Meditation 7 The Healing Light Above
Side B—Meditation 8 Be Open to Receive Light

VOLUME II   REMEMBERING WHO YOU ARE

ISBN 1-930455-33-X $75/set

Once your mind has been cleared in Volume I, you have the opportunity for Volume II to help you bring forth the remembrance of who you are. Once you remember, there's no higher platform; you are in touch with all your powers, spontaneously and effortlessly. It is important to *master* this second volume so you can TRUST yourself to leave your body as you journey to save souls.

Tape 1
Side A—Meditation 9   Meet the Self Within
Side B—Meditation 10 Going Home to the Self Inside

Tape 2
Side A—Meditation 11 Acknowledging Your Body
Side B—Meditation 12 Give Up Doing, and Be

Tape 3
Side A—Meditation 13 You Are the Light of the World
Side B—Meditation 14 Finding Your Soul's Purpose in Life

Tape 4
Side A—Meditation 15 Release and Let Go of the Past
Side B—Meditation 16 You Are Worthy and Deserving

ADVANCED MEDITATION
A JOURNEY FROM BODY TO SPIRIT

VOLUME III   OUT-OF-BODY AND SAVING SOULS

ISBN 1-930455-34-8 $75/set

Now that you have completed Volume II and have total trust, you are ready for Volume III, which teaches you to leave your physical body at will, and save the lost souls of loved ones.

Tape 1
Side A—Meditation 17 Preparing for Out-of-Body Experience
Side B—Meditation 18 Leaving Your Body #1

Tape 2
Side A—Meditation 19 Leaving Your Body #2
Side B—Meditation 20 Leaving Your Body #3

Tape 3
Side A—Meditation 21 Visit the Angels
Side B—Meditation 22 Know the Different Realms of Being

Tape 4
Side A—Meditation 23 Saving the Lost Souls
Side B—Meditation 24 More Soul Saving

VOLUME IV   ASTRAL TRAVELING

ISBN 1-930455-35-6 $75/set

Now that you have completed Volume III and it is comfortable and effortless for you to leave your body, I invite you to join my angel companions and me in the joy of astral travel.

Tape 1
Side A—Meditation 25 Contacting an Alien Mother-Ship
Side B—Meditation 26 Journey to the Deep Sea

Tape 2
Side A—Meditation 27 An Advanced and Peaceful Being
Side B—Meditation 28 Stone-Age Earth

Tape 3
Side A—Meditation 29 An Advanced Mental Planet
Side B—Meditation 30 Journey Through Mind and Body

Tape 4
Side A—Meditation 31 The Lowest Energy in the Universe
Side B—Meditation 32 The Highest Energy in the Universe

Prices not include shipping and handling charges.

186

ADVANCED MEDITATION
WITH BIJAN

A
Journey
from Body to Spirit

Bijan's voice vibrates in a full frequency of limitlessness,
and brings your soul's tuning fork to the same vibration.

Each time
that you listen to Bijan's voice in these meditations
you will go deeper and deeper in your subconscious mind.

Each time
that you listen to each meditation,
it will be easier for you
to get in touch with your Source.

If You Are Ready,
You Will Know

TSAM SPEC   Advanced Meditation Tapesets I-IV — $275

Each meditation tape is a foundation and support for the next,
and along the way each tape will teach patience and giving up control.

Listen to each meditation tape as many times as is comfortable for you—
and let go of judging and comparing.

Understand that you must
live each tape in Volume I for II to be effective;
live each tape in Volume II for III to be effective;
live each tape in Volume III for IV to be effective.

187

VISITED THE WEBSITE LATELY?
JOIN US AT
www.effortlessprosperity.com

Enjoying the online seminar?
www.effortlessprosperity.com/seminar
The daily lessons of *Absolutely Effortless Prosperity, Book* I have been on the website since 1997—so that people from all over the world have the opportunity to "read from the same page" each day, no matter where they live, even if they cannot access the actual book. It is Bijan's gift to everyone on this planet, so we may create world peace. We invite you to visit the on-line seminar, where you can read the day's lesson, assignment and story—and we encourage you to pass it on to your friends worldwide!

Seeking a Study Group?
Or have you formed a miracle-sharing group with other light-minded people? Let us know if you've created one in your area. Call, write or email *groups@effortlessprosperity.com*. For an updated listing of groups worldwide, check often at *www.effortlessprosperity.com/studygroup*

Would you like to be part of a worldwide miracle-sharing group?
miracles-happen-subscribe@yahoo.com
You are invited to join our internet miracle-sharing group, where you can e-mail your own miracles and receive the daily digest of joyful sharing from people in all parts of the world. The miracle digest is truly a dose of sunshine!

Interested in hearing or seeing Bijan in person?
For updates on Bijan's schedule of radio and TV appearances, seminars and workshops, check often at *www.effortlessprosperity.com/inperson*.
To host a book-signing, seminar or workshop in your area, call toll-free at 800-437-7750 or email *bijan@effortlessprosperity.com*

Are you ready for Effortless Success Coaching?
Take the test at *www.effortlessprosperity.com/coaching*—or call for details.

The product listing in this catalog is current as of March 2001. If you would like to check to see what's new from Bijan, check often at www.effortlessprosperity.com/publishing

CREATE A STUDY GROUP

Two people who are vigilant for the light
are much more powerful than hundreds of people
living in darkness.

A STUDY GROUP IS...

An Effortless Prosperity Study Group consists of two or more people who come together to grow in the light and share miracles. It is a thirty-day program that begins on the first day of the month and concludes on the thirtieth day, with a celebration.

- Each meeting begins with the joining of hands in a circle as one of the participants—or a facilitator—says a few words to bring the group together in spirit.
- This is followed by the reading of the day's lesson and assignment, or by listening to Bijan's tape for the day from the *Book I* or *Book II* companion tape set. The remainder of the meeting is filled with the sharing of miracles.
- Giving is receiving and receiving is giving—in many groups, a donation basket is passed around before the close of each meeting, and at the end of the month, the groups use the money to create joy and make miracles happen through charitable acts.
- The meeting is brought to a close with a joining of hands as .a facilitator or one of the participants says a few words.

An Effortless Prosperity study group is a gathering place of joy, peace, light and love. It is not a therapy session, a 12-step program, or a religious meeting—it is simply a place to gather for the purpose of sharing miracles of the day. Because of this, study groups are adaptable to every imaginable environment—home, the workplace, the gym, church groups, senior centers, detention centers, hospitals—wherever there are people.

In a study group there is no preaching or advising, nor is there networking or business talk; darkness is never shared, nor are long stories that often invite it. Sharing miracles is most important. The effect is so powerful that eventually those in the group will begin to share miracles with everyone they meet, and will begin to notice the light in everything they do. Miraculously, their lives will be transformed—they will see people differently; relationships will either become joyful or they will end for the best interest of all; they will feel healthy and happy for no particular reason, and will experience abundance in their lives.

189

Effortless Prosperity study groups all over the world follow these guidelines—and as every group focuses on the same lesson on the same day of the month, each of us aligns with the collective consciousness of all our sisters and brothers in the light. There is tremendous power and effectiveness that comes forth when so many people around the world are doing the same lesson on the same day. The global and personal benefits of Effortless Prosperity multiply greatly.

FACILITATING...

Facilitating a study group is both fun and enlightening; it can be a source of great joy and inspiration in your life, and need not consume much of your time or energy. All that is required for starting your own group is the desire to open more to joy and peace, and the desire to share joy and peace with others. When you simply create the space for people to join together, read the day's lesson, and share your own shifts in perception, you will open the other participants to becoming aware of the miracles in their own lives. It can be the one place where everyone leaves all problems outside the door and is enveloped in the light!

AS YOU CREATE A STUDY GROUP...

We'd love to hear about it! You can let us know by phone, fax, or mail, or drop us a line at **groups@effortlessprosperity.com.** Let us know your name, address, city and state, the time of day that you meet, and any other pertinent information about your group. We plan on posting a list of ongoing study groups worldwide.

AND SEND US YOUR MIRACLES!

Has your life changed since studying the *Effortless Prosperity* books? Do you have some miracles you would like to share with the world? Has your study group created some magnificent miracles in your community? We are in the process of assembling the first book of a series, called **Miracles Happen!** If you would like to empower others by including your personal miracles and testimonials in this book, please send them to us, completing and signing the form on page 133. If one of your miracles is selected to be included in the *Miracles Happen!* series, we'll send you an autographed copy in appreciation.

Special Note: Your personal miracles can only be considered if they are accompanied by the signed release. All submissions will become the property of Effortless Prosperity, Inc. Thank-you!

ABOUT BIJAN

Bijan Anjomi is a man who is making a difference. Author, speaker, founder of Effortless Prosperity Seminars, success coach and a visionary for world peace, he lectures internationally in the fields of health, spirituality and spontaneous living.

Born in Persia and raised as a student of the Baha'i, Judaic and Muslim faiths, Bijan came to the United States when he was 19 years old. In the years that followed, his natural curiosity led him along many paths. To name a few, he owned a health club—worked as a bartender, maitre 'd and a bouncer in bars—attended college—became a commercial real estate agent—studied various forms of meditation—attained his certification as a clinical hypnotherapist—and captured the title of Mr. Universe, Natural Division for 1993 and 1994.

The evolution of Bijan-the-author began in the late 1980's, when he began studying, practicing and finally teaching the principles set forth in *A Course In Miracles*. Over the next nine years, he noticed that his life was gradually changing for the better; by the mid-90's, his health was flawless, his relationships were joyful and harmonious, and all that he desired was being provided without effort. At this point, his higher consciousness—or "guide", as Bijan refers to him—appeared, and asked him to write a book called *Absolutely Effortless Prosperity*. Bijan admits that he was, to put it mildly, not very receptive to the idea, as he had never found reading or writing to be a particularly joyful activity. Regardless, he finally agreed to write the book. The first edition of *Absolutely Effortless Prosperity* was self-published in February of 1997 for a small group of people who were invited to be part of a thirty-day seminar. Within a month, the Las Vegas Effortless Prosperity Center opened, and study groups were meeting every two hours from morning 'til night, seven days a week. And then, through miracles and word-of-mouth, this simple book of thirty lessons was falling into the hands of people everywhere.

In the next two years, Bijan hosted his own radio show in Las Vegas, appeared on radio and TV talk shows in Los Angeles, San Francisco, Las Vegas and New York, and became a regular guest on WOR New York's nationally-syndicated *Joey Reynolds Show*. He was further guided to bring forth a series of books for children and teenagers, a book on health, and the next set of lessons for adults—all following the basic principles of *Absolutely Effortless Prosperity*.

Through the guidance of his higher consciousness, he has been directed to manifest his works for one purpose: world peace. The purpose of his books, tapes, seminars and workshops is to assist people in opening their hearts to joy and peace—experiencing and believing in it, and living in the reality of it.

To this end, Bijan continues reaching out to people worldwide, through speaking engagements, television, radio, personal coaching, and through his website. He has guided many students of his original classes to go forth as study group facilitators in prisons, shelters and dependency groups, and has watched the blossoming of the programs for children. As more and more employers are beginning to schedule meditation or "spirituality breaks" for their employees, he is also hearing news about study groups in the workplace. The light of Effortless Prosperity is steadily growing brighter and stronger, as people step forth to translate the writings into other languages: the Spanish edition of *Prosperidad Sin Esfuerzo* has been in Mexico since 1998, the Persian(farsi) translation was introduced in early 2000, while French, Italian, Dutch, Chinese, Japanese and Polish translations are in process.

Bijan's vision is simple yet profound. The basic truth is these words he speaks, time and again: *"As more and more people begin to experience joyful, peaceful, abundant living, the barriers between countries, cultures and religious philosophies will simply melt away."*

MIRACLE SHARE

Always remember Bijan's Law:
Everything that CAN go right, WILL go right.
EXPECT MIRACLES!

In the space below and on the following page, please write down the growth you have experienced since you have been participating in Effortless Prosperity, and share some of your favorite miracles with us. Attach additional sheets if necessary. Effortless Prosperity reserves the right to abbreviate or modify your story for the purposes of publication.

I am happy to give permission to Effortless Prosperity to share all or part of my testimonial and miracles with the world!

Print Full Name_____

Signature_____Date_____

Phone_____

EFFORTLESS ORDER FORM

Qty	Item	Description	$US/CAN	Total
	BA1	**Book** - Absolutely Effortless Prosperity Book I	$15/$22	
	BA1Farsi	**Book** - Absolutely Effortless Prosperity - Farsi	$12/$18	
	T Aff Farsi	**Tape** - Affirmations in Farsi	$10/$15	
	TS BA1	**Tape** - Book I 16-tape set	$75/$110	
	Bmk1	**Bmk** - Bookmark, Book I	$1/$1.50	
	Bmk1 Spec	**Bmk** - Bookmark, Book I 12-pack Special	$10/$15	
	BA2	**Book** - Absolutely Effortless Prosperity Book II	$15/$22	
	TS BA2	**Tape** - Book II 16-tape set	$75/$110	
	TS Rec1	**Tape** - How To Be Open To Receive - Vol I	$35/$52	
	TS Rec2	**Tape** - How To Be Open To Receive - Vol II	$35/$52	
	BH	**Book** - The Common Sense of Effortless Health	$10/$15	
	T Health	**Tape** - Effortless Health	$10/$15	
	T Laf	**Tape** - Effortless Laughter w/affirmations	$10/$15	
	T Affirm	**Tape** - Effortless Affirmations For Everyone	$10/$15	
	T Med	**Tape** - Meditation	$8/$10	
	TS AM1	**Tape** - Advanced Meditation Volume I (2001)	$75/$110	
	TS AM2	**Tape** - Advanced Meditation Volume II (2001)	$75/$110	
	TS AM3	**Tape** - Advanced Meditation Volume III (2001)	$75/$110	
	TS AM4	**Tape** - Advanced Meditation Volume IV (2001)	$75/$110	
	TS AM Spec	**Tape** - Advanced Meditation Vols. I-IV (2001)	$275/$404	
	T Job	**Tape** - Having an Effortless and Joyous Job	$10/$15	
	T Giv	**Tape** - Giving & Receiving	$10/$15	
	T Mast	**Tape** - Attain Mastery	$10/$15	
	T Man	**Tape** - Manifesting Consciously (2001)	$10/$15	
	CD Man	**CD - Manifesting Consciously**	$15/$22	
	T Heal	**Tape** - Healing in the New Millennium (2001)	$10/$15	
	CD Heal	**CD - Healing in the New Millennium**	$15/$22	
	BC1	**Book** - Little Friends Of Nature, Book I (2-7)	$10/$15	
	BC2	**Book** - Little Friends Of Nature, Book II (2-7)	$10/$15	*
	BY1	**Book** - My Guiding Spirit, Book I (8-12)	$10/$15	
	BY2	**Book** - My Guiding Spirit, Book II (8-12)	$10/$15	*
	BT1	**Book** - Light From The Sky, Book I (13-18)	$10/$15	
	BT2	**Book** - Light From The Sky, Book II (13-18)	$10/$15	*

Shipping & Handling Rates		Subtotal	
Up to $50 - $5.00	$101 - $150 - $15.00	Shipping & Handling	
$51 - $100 - $10.00	$151 - $240 - $20.00		
* check for availability		NV residents add 7.25% sales tax	
		Total	

195

EFFORTLESS ORDER FORM

TOLL FREE 1-800-437-7750 & have your credit card ready.
On-line orders: www.effortlessprosperity.com/publishing
Mail orders: Effortless Prosperity, Inc. P.O. Box 370703, Las Vegas NV 89137
Phone: 702-735-6559 Fax: 702-254-0095

☐   I have enclosed a check or money order
payable to Effortless Prosperity

I am paying by:

☐ VISA   ☐ MasterCard   ☐ Discover   ☐ American Express
☐Other _____

Number: ___ ___ ___ ___-___ ___ ___ ___-___ ___ ___ ___-___ ___ ___ ___

Expiration date: _____/_____

Signature:_____

Billing address if different from below_____

Ship To:

Name: _____
Shipping Address: _____Apt./Unit No:_____
City:_____ State:_____ Zip+ 4:_____ -_____
Day Phone: _____-_____Evening Phone: _____-_____

☐   I would like to be on your mailing list & receive your free newsletter.

☐   My e-mail address is:_____

☐   I have a website and it's at:_____

Prices subject to change without notice.
Please call or write for volume discounts.